Hummingbirds

Hummingbirds

Text by **RONALD ORENSTEIN**

Photography by **MICHAEL and PATRICIA FOGDEN**

FIREFLY BOOKS

A FIREFLY BOOK

Copyright © 2014 Firefly Books Ltd.
Text copyright © 2014 Ronald Orenstein
Photographs and accompanying captions copyright © 2014
Michael and Patricia Fogden (unless otherwise noted)
page 8 © Rolf Nussbaumer/Nature Picture Library
page 26 © Takahashi Photography/Shutterstock
page 60 © Bert Willaert/Nature Picture Library
page 66 © Peter Hodum/Oikonos

First Printing

For my mother, MARY ORENSTEIN
(who has always appreciated beauty).
And to the memory of my grandmother, RUTH MONNES (1899–1974),
(who first showed me a hummingbird).

The publisher gratefully acknowledges the financial
support for our publishing program by the Government of
Canada through the Canada Book Fund as administered
by the Department of Canadian Heritage.

Publisher Cataloging-in-Publication Data (U.S.)
Orenstein, Ronald.
   Hummingbirds / text by Ronald Orenstein ;
photography by Michael and Patricia Fogden.
[256] pages : col. photos. ; cm.
Includes bibliographical references and index.
ISBN-13: 978-1-77085-400-0
1. Hummingbirds. I. Fogden, Michael. II. Fogden,
Patricia. III. Title.
598.764 dc 23   QL696.A558.O645 2014

**Library and Archives Canada Cataloguing in
Publication**
Orenstein, Ronald I. (Ronald Isaac), 1946-, author
       Hummingbirds / Ronald Orenstein.
Includes bibliographical references and index.
ISBN 978-1-77085-400-0 (bound)
       1. Hummingbirds. I. Title.
QL696.A558O74 2014   598.7'64   C2014-901156-3

Published in the United States by
Firefly Books (U.S.) Inc.
P.O. Box 1338, Ellicott Station
Buffalo, New York 14205

Design by Jacqueline Hope Raynor

Printed in China

Published in Canada by
Firefly Books Ltd.
50 Staples Avenue, Unit 1
Richmond Hill, Ontario L4B 0A7

Right: Violet-tailed Sylph (*Aglaiocercus coelestis*)
Previous page: Chestnut-breasted Coronet (*Boissonneaua matthewsii*)

Acknowledgments

First of all, my thanks to Michael Worek and Firefly Books, for the opportunity to work on this project, to Pippa Kennard of Firefly for her patient editorial help, and to Michael and Patricia Fogden for allowing me to share the space between these covers with their beautiful photographs.

I owe thanks to Christopher J. Clark, Gunnar Engblom, Francisco E. Fontúrbel, Susan Healy, Richard Klim, Nancy L. Newfield, Donald R. Powers, Laurent Raty, Alejandro Rico-Guevara and Ethan J. Temeles, all of whom read and commented on portions of the text.

My particular thanks to F. Gary Stiles, both for that wonderful morning netting Costa Rican hummingbirds back in 1971, and for his generous and valuable editorial comments on the whole manuscript. In addition to notes and corrections, Gary kindly supplied me with fascinating information and insights from his own research, some still unpublished. I have done my best to incorporate them here, but any errors or misunderstandings remain mine.

Much of this book was written in Kuching, Malaysia. I owe a special thank you to my stepdaughter Fiona Marcus Raja, for helping me with various drafts when my laptop refused to speak the local printer dialect, and to Ryan, Royce and Ryder for occasionally letting Grandpa get some work done!

Finally, as always, thanks beyond measure to my wife, Eileen Yen Ee Lee, without whom this book might not exist (and without whom I might not have much reason to exist myself).

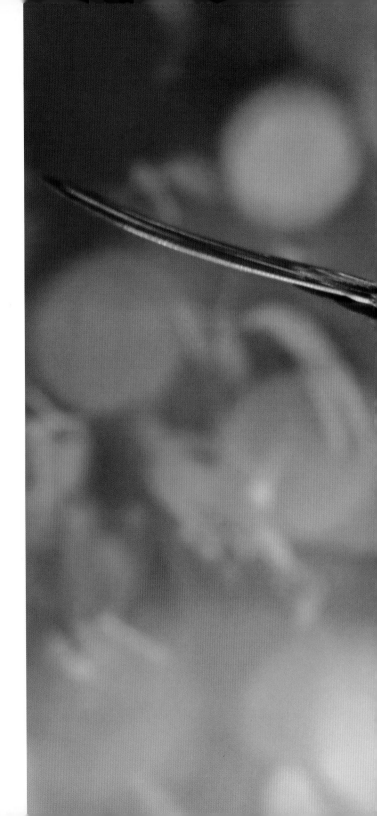

Velvet-purple Coronet (*Boissonneaua jardini*)

Contents

Acknowledgments   6

Foreword   9

Chapter 1:   The Most Extraordinary Birds   13

Chapter 2:   How Hummingbirds Evolved   17

Chapter 3:   How Hummingbirds Fly   27

Chapter 4:   How Hummingbirds Refuel   31

Chapter 5:   How Hummingbirds Glow   47

Chapter 6:   The World of the Hummingbird   51

Chapter 7:   A Future for Hummingbirds   65

Portfolio of Images   71

Further Reading   251

Index   253

The author's first tropical hummingbird: a male Red-billed Streamertail (*Trochilus polytmus*), the bird Victorian naturalist Philip Henry Gosse called "the gem of Jamaican ornithology."

Foreword

In 1957, when I was 10 years old, our family moved to Jamaica, where my father and mother worked together to build one of the first modern resort hotels on the island. For a bookish child interested in natural history, it was a journey to paradise. I was suddenly in a new and brilliant world, full of all sorts of fascinating creatures. Nothing brought that home to me more than a tiny, impossibly exotic bird. Its body glowed emerald-green. Its bill shone brilliant red and its tail stretched out into two extraordinary, frilled black ribbons, longer than the bird itself. I couldn't imagine what it was. I finally found its name in May Jeffrey-Smith's delightful *Bird-Watching in Jamaica*: Long-Tail Doctor Bird, named for its needle of a bill. Today ornithologists call it the Red-billed Streamertail (*Trochilus polytmus*). It was my first tropical hummingbird.

It was not my first hummingbird. That was a Ruby-throated Hummingbird (*Archilochus colubris*) that my grandmother showed me as it hovered among the flowers near our summer cottage in Ontario. I think, though, that it was the Streamertail that focused my childhood interest in animals on the beauty and diversity of birds.

A few years later, as a teenager, I received a treasured gift from my grandparents: a copy of Crawford H. Greenewalt's remarkable *Hummingbirds* (1960), the seminal modern book on the family. Greenewalt was not an ornithologist, but a chemical engineer who rose to be president and CEO of DuPont. He was a pioneer in high-speed flash photography. I remember my excitement as I leafed through his razor-sharp photographs, hand-tipped into the book, showing 65 species of hummingbird (including a spectacular cover photo of my beloved Red-billed Streamertail). What amazing, gorgeous creatures these were!

A decade after that, I found myself on a graduate field study program in Costa Rica. Here was a veritable blizzard of hummingbirds: a Long-billed Hermit (*Phaethornis longirostris*) whirring unobtrusively along its chosen path through the rainforest undergrowth; a White-necked Jacobin (*Florisuga mellivora*) showing off his flashing white collar and tail feathers in repeated display flights, sallying 40 feet (12 m) in the air and back again for the benefit of an unseen female; a Long-billed Starthroat (*Heliomaster longirostris*) vigorously defending the scarlet blossoms of an *Erythrina* tree against all comers; a Fiery-throated Hummingbird (*Panterpe insignis*), high on the Pan-American Highway, zooming to within a foot of me, apparently mistaking my bright red sweater for a flower. After the program ended, my good friend and fellow naturalist Barry Kent Mackay and I spent a memorable morning in a heliconia grove at the La Selva field station on the Caribbean slope, carefully picking some 80 hummingbirds, of well over a dozen species, out of strategically placed mist nets for a study by Dr. Gary Stiles and Dr. Larry Wolf. The birds, I hasten to add, were marked with dabs of paint for later recognition, wondered over, and released unharmed.

In the ensuing years I have been lucky enough to encounter, and marvel at, hummingbirds across the breadth of their range, from flower-filled meadows in the Rockies to damp, dark beech forests in southern Chile. I have spent hours surrounded by hummers in bewildering variety, at feeders in southern Brazil and southeastern Peru. I have seen the largest of them all, the Giant Hummingbird (*Patagona gigas*), in the Andes, and waded through Cuba's Zapata Swamp in (successful) search of the smallest, the Bee Hummingbird (*Mellisuga helenae*), with the remarkable Orestes Martinez Garcia (known to birders as "el Chino de Zapata"). Though in recent years I have done most of my tropical birding in my wife's home country of Malaysia (where, I keep having to explain, hummingbirds do not occur), hummingbirds remain — unsurprisingly — among my favorite creatures.

The chance to write the text for this book, therefore, came as a particular pleasure — especially for the honor of accompanying its magnificent series of photographs by the deans of hummingbird photography, Michael and Patricia Fogden. There are many books about hummingbirds, and I wanted to make this one a bit different. Rather than turn out yet another general natural history of the hummingbird family, I have made the theme of this book the things that make these extraordinary creatures unique among birds. To do that, I have focused on the most recent scientific research into their relationships, their lives and their chances for survival. Much of this information has not, to my knowledge, appeared in any book for the general reader.

In the past few years, scientists have used high-speed videography, field experiments and computer modeling to understand just how hummingbirds are able to do some of the highly demanding and difficult things they do. We are uncovering the secrets of how they hover, motionless and seemingly without effort, in mid-air, how they find and remember the locations of hundreds of flowers, how their tongues draw nectar from a flower, how they snap up flying insects in a fraction of a second and how they make sounds not just with their voices, but with their tails. These and other discoveries form the core of this book, and I hope readers will find them as fascinating as I do.

A technical note: the names I use for hummingbirds found in North America (including Central America and the West Indies) follow the online version of the American Ornithologists' Union Checklist of North and Middle American Birds (checklist.aou.org/taxa/) as of March 1, 2014, except that I recognize two species of streamertail in Jamaica, the Red-billed Streamertail (*Trochilus polytmus*) and the Black-billed Streamertail (*T. scitulus*) instead of one. For South American species not in the AOU Checklist, I follow the International Ornithological Congress World Bird List (IOC, Gill, F & D Donsker. IOC World Bird List [v 4.1], IOC. doi : 10.14344/IOC.ML.4.1). A complete list of references can be downloaded from my blog at http://ronorensteinwriter.blogspot.ca/2014/06/reference-list-for-hummingbirds.html.

Little Woodstar (*Chaetocercus bombus*)

ONE

The Most Extraordinary Birds

If there are more extraordinary birds than hummingbirds — those exotic creatures the Brazilians call *beija-flores*, flower-kissers — it is difficult to imagine what they might be. No other birds fly with their precision and aerial mobility. None live at the extreme metabolic pace that sets hummingbirds apart not just from birds, but from all other vertebrates. That tiny gem in your garden — should you live in the Americas, where all hummingbirds are found today — is a marvel.

Certainly the people who first encountered them thought so. Hummingbirds feature prominently in the pre-Columbian art and lore of the Americas. Native Americans saw, and still see, them as healers, as messengers from the spirit world and as omens of good luck. Talismans made from dried hummingbirds or their nests are still worn or carried as lucky charms or guarantees of love in Mexico, Costa Rica and other Latin American countries. For native hunters and travelers in the Pacific Northwest, the hummingbird is a benevolent guide, able to fly backwards should its followers fall behind. To the Squamish of British Columbia, the hummingbird symbolizes beauty, intelligence and love. Its image appears on totem poles. One of the mysterious figures on the Nazca Plains of Peru probably depicts a gigantic, stylized hummingbird.

The Aztecs, impressed by the brilliance and territorial ferocity of hummingbirds, saw them as symbols of a deity. Huītzilopōchtli (literally "hummingbird of the south" or "hummingbird on the left"), was their god of war, the sun and human sacrifice, as well as the patron deity of their capital city, Tenochtitlan. Warriors who died in battle went to join Huītzilopōchtli, following the sun on its path through the heavens. After four years the warriors returned to earth, having been transformed into hummingbirds (or, sometimes, butterflies), to feed on nectar for all eternity.

To the Mayans a hummingbird was the sun in disguise, seeking to court the moon. Other Mayan legends tell of how the Great Spirit created hummingbirds out of the colored scraps left over from the creation of other birds while the sun added its brilliance as a special gift, or of how all the other birds gave the hummingbird Tzunuum their brightest feathers to wear on his wedding day, and the Great Spirit allowed him to wear them forever after. The Kogui of Colombia believe that a hummingbird gave mankind the gift of fire.

Sword-billed Hummingbird
(*Ensifera ensifera*)

The Cherokee tell of a hummingbird that raced a crane around the world for seven days for the love of a beautiful woman. He was by far the faster flyer, but like Aesop's hare he took time out to sleep along the way. The crane continued around the clock, repeatedly passing the sleeping hummingbird by night, and won the race (the beautiful woman, who preferred the hummingbird, stayed single). The tellers of this tale knew their hummingbirds: active as they are in flight, hummingbirds spend most of their daylight hours resting and may fall, at night, into a state of deep torpor.

Europeans had to wait until post-Columbian times to see their first hummingbird. As early as 1518, the Spaniard Martín Fernández de Enciso (c. 1470–1528), who had traveled twice to the Paria region of what is now Venezuela, wrote in his *Suma de Geographia* of birds "no bigger of bodie than the tope of a man's thumb but they have the goodliest colored feathers that ever man might see" (from a 1541 English translation). In 1525, Gonzalo Fernández de Oviedo (1478–1557) remarked in his *Hystoria General de las Indias* on a creature the natives of Hispaniola called the *paxaro mosquito* or mosquito bird. Oviedo was perhaps referring to the Vervain Hummingbird (*Mellisuga minima*), the second-smallest bird in the world.

The *Historia General de las Cosas de Nueva España*, a manuscript assembled between 1550 and 1585 by Franciscan missionary Bernardino de Sahagún, contains the earliest unequivocal drawing of hummingbirds in Europe. Sahagún's text, based on interviews with elderly Aztecs who remembered the times before the conquest, describes nine species of hummingbirds. It notes, accurately, that they feed on "flower dew" and lay no more than two eggs per clutch. It also records the odd belief that during the winter the birds stick their bills into branches and die, but revive in spring clothed in bright new plumage. Perhaps the Aztecs had found dead birds mummified in place on their perches, something that can indeed happen after a cold spell.

The name "hummingbird," or something like it, was already in use by the early 17th century. William Wood enthused about the Ruby-throated Hummingbird (*Archilochus colubris*) in his *New England's Prospect* (1634), a guide for prospective settlers: "The Humbird is one of the wonders of the Countrey, being no bigger than a Hornet, yet hath all the demensions of a Bird, as bill, and wings, with quills, spider-like legges, small clawes : For color, she is as glorious as the Raine-bow; as she flies, she makes a little humming noise like a Humble-bee: wherefore shee is called the Humbird."

In his *New English Canaan* (1637) — a political tract that may have been written with the assistance of no less than Ben Jonson — Thomas Morton extolled the Ruby-throated Hummingbird's beauty but thought it ate bees rather than nectar: "There is a curious bird to see to, called a hunning bird, no bigger than a great Beetle; that out of question lives upon the Bee, which he eateth and catcheth amongst Flowers: For it is his Custome to frequent those places, Flowers hee cannot feed upon by reason of his sharp bill, which is like the poynt of a Spannish needle, but shorte. His fethers have a glasse like silke, and as hee stirres, they shew to be of a chaingable coloure: and has bin, and is admired for shape coloure, and size."

Europeans continued, over the next few centuries, to load hummingbirds with superlatives. Georges-Louis Leclerc, Comte de Buffon, wrote in volume 11 of his *Histoire naturelle des oiseaux* (*Natural History of Birds*) (1770–1786): "Of all animated beings, here is the most elegant in form and the most brilliant in color. The stones and metals polished by our art are not comparable to this gem of Nature. The emerald, the ruby, the topaz shine in his costume." Buffon's description became a frequently plagiarized classic, and emerald, ruby and topaz remain English names of a number of hummingbirds today.

John Keats inverted Buffon's comparison, writing in his poem *On receiving a curious Shell* of "a gem/ … Bright as the humming-bird's green diadem, / When it flutters in sun-beams that shine through a fountain." Alexander Wilson (1766-1813), Scottish ornithologist, poet, artist, older contemporary of Audubon and pioneer chronicler of the birds of North America, rhapsodized about the beauty of hummingbird plumage in his poem *Dawn* (*The Humming-Bird*), while noting with a naturalist's eye (as Morton did) that their iridescent colors cannot be seen from every angle: "What heavenly tints in mingling radiance fly;/ Each rapid movement gives a different dye;/ Like scales of burnish'd gold, they dazzling show,/ Now sink to shade — now like a furnace glow!"

Nineteenth-century Europeans expressed their fascination with hummingbirds less in poetry and more by importing millions of their dead bodies. Stuffed hummingbirds were prized for everything from women's hats and feather ornaments to exhibits under glass domes and collectors' curio cabinets. One London dealer reportedly imported 400,000 dead hummingbirds in a single year from Bogotá, Colombia, a transhipment point for vast numbers of bird specimens. The Bogotá Sunangel (*Heliangelus zusii*) is still known for certain only from a "Bogotá skin." There are other unique "Bogotá hummingbirds," but most probably represent hybrids rather than lost species. Even the Bogotá Sunangel may be a hybrid.

Hummingbirds are found on Trinidad and Tobago's coat of arms, but Trinidad may owe its old name "Land of the Hummingbird" to the huge number of skins from South America that were shipped to European markets via the island in the late 19th and early 20th centuries. A total of 37,603 hummingbird skins from South America and Trinidad were once auctioned in a single sale, and an 1892 order from a London milliner included 40,000 hummingbird feathers. It is a testimony to hummingbird abundance and fecundity that most species seem to have survived the European craving for them.

Our interest in hummingbirds continues, less lethally, today. They have been the subject of countless books. A copy of the most famous of them, John Gould's mid-19th century, multi-volume *A Monograph of the Trochilidae, or Family of Humming-Birds*, sold at Christies in 2011 for 151,000 Euros (US$217,845), making it one of the most valuable bird books ever written. Gould used real gold leaf on his hand-colored plates, overpainted with transparent oils and varnish, in an attempt to illustrate the iridescent colors of his subjects. For hummingbirds, nothing but the best would do.

TWO

How Hummingbirds Evolved

Ornithologists place hummingbirds in their own family, the Trochilidae. Molecular studies have confirmed the long-held idea that their nearest relatives are the highly aerial swifts (Apodidae) and the swifts' southeast Asian and Australasian cousins the treeswifts (Hemiprocnidae). Their next-nearest relatives appear to be the nocturnal owlet-nightjars (Aegothelidae) of Australia, New Guinea and nearby islands. Swifts, treeswifts and hummingbirds make up the order Apodiformes, or footless birds. Of course hummingbirds have feet, but they are short, weak and almost useless for anything except sitting on a perch (swifts can't even do that), shuffling a bit, or scratching themselves. Apodiform birds, instead, are superb flyers. Whether aerial darts like the swifts, or miniature helicopters like the hummingbirds, they have evolved for life on the wing.

The small, pale shapes seen at the base of this Purple-bibbed Whitetip's (*Urosticte benjamini*) bill are flower mites hitching a lift between the flowers on which they live and feed. When a hummingbird's bill appears in a flower the mites wish to leave, they rapidly climb on board and survive the flight by traveling within the bird's nostrils. When they detect that they have arrived at another favored flower, they leave their sanctuary and hurry down the hummingbird's bill into their new home while the bird feeds.

Hummingbirds and swifts (including treeswifts) may have gone their separate evolutionary ways over 70 million years ago, well before the fall of the dinosaurs. Oddly enough, these quintessentially American birds may have gotten their start in Europe. We have known for some decades that there were once birds in Europe intermediate between swifts and hummingbirds, combining an early version of a hummingbird's hovering wing with the short beak and broad gape of a swift. They may be evidence that hummingbird ancestors took to hovering before they began to probe flowers for nectar, perhaps to pluck insects from a leaf or a blossom.

About 10 years ago, scientists found the first fossils of an unquestionable European hummingbird. They named it *Eurotrochilus inexpectatus*, which means "unexpected hummingbird from Europe." It was about the size of a modern Rufous-breasted Hermit (*Glaucis hirsuta*) and appears to have been quite common in the early Oligocene, about 32 million years ago. Specimens have been found in Germany and France, and the remains of another *Eurotrochilus* species have been unearthed in Poland.

Eurotrochilus had a long, slender bill like that of its modern relatives. It lacked some of the structural modifications that enable modern hummingbirds to hover and feed on nectar, and it may not have been able to do either with the efficacy of its modern cousins. Though *Eurotrochilus* may have fed on flying insects instead, it raises the intriguing possibility that some flowers in the Old World, pollinated today by sunbirds or long-tongued bees, may have originally evolved in partnership with early hummingbirds that have long vanished from their original homeland.

Modern hummingbirds are fantastically specialized nectar-feeding machines, but they are not the only nectarivores (feeders on nectar) in the avian world. The lories, nectar-feeding parrots from Australasia, lap up pollen and nectar with brush-tipped tongues, as do a few other parrots. Other nectarivore families belong to the vast order Passeriformes, or perching birds. They include the sunbirds (Nectariniidae), a large assemblage of colorful songbirds from Africa, Asia and northern Australia, and the honeyeaters (Meliphagidae), one of the dominant bird families of Australia and New Guinea. The two false-sunbirds (*Neodrepanis* spp.) of Madagascar are nectarivore members of an ancient perching-bird lineage. In the Hawaiian Islands there were once two groups of nectar-feeding songbirds, the Hawaiian finches (Drepanidini) and the now-extinct 'O'os (Mohoidae), long thought to be honeyeaters but now known to be related to waxwings (Bombycillidae). In tropical America, honeycreepers (*Cyanerpes* and *Chlorophanes*), flower-piercers (*Diglossa*) and the Bananaquit (*Coereba flaveola*) live alongside hummingbirds. Many other birds, from a range of families, will take nectar when they can get it, but no other bird has evolved the hummingbird's extreme specialization for hovering flight, or its hyperactive, sugar-fueled metabolism. If other birds are, nonetheless, successful nectar-feeders, why have hummingbirds become so extreme?

Lories and nectar-feeding songbirds are highly acrobatic, able to twist and turn from their perches to reach out-of-the-way flowers. Hummingbirds, however, evolved from birds that had lost much of their ability to move around, except in the air. When a brooding hummingbird turns around on her nest, she does so not with her feet but by flying upwards, spinning around in the air and settling again. When a Bearded Helmetcrest (*Oxypogon guerinii*) I was observing hunting insects on the ground in Venezuela moved even a tiny distance, instead of walking or hopping like any other bird, it flew.

As hummingbirds specialized in feeding at flowers, it may have been easier (in an evolutionary sense) for them to become extreme hoverers rather than to re-acquire acrobatic legs and feet. By doing so, they may have guaranteed themselves access to floral resources that perching nectar-feeders could not reach. Hovering hummingbirds can visit flowers growing on stems too weak to bear their weight. Nectar-feeding songbirds generally feed on the flowers of trees and shrubs or the more solidly built herbaceous plants (gingers, for example). One recent study has suggested that, in the American tropics, nectar-feeding songbirds may be more important pollinators in the rainforest canopy than hummingbirds.

But hummingbirds do sometimes perch to feed. The peculiar sicklebills (*Eutoxeres* spp.) cling to the flowers of heliconias while probing them for nectar, probably because it is easier to insert a deeply curved bill into a flower from a perch. Hummingbirds that live in páramo and puna, the lands above the tree line in the Andes, tend to have larger and stronger feet than their relatives that live at lower elevations. Perching is a much less costly way to feed at flowers amid the thin air and cold winds of the high country.

Hummingbirds Conquer the Americas

Today, hummingbirds are found only in the Americas, though the most northerly of them, the highly migratory Rufous Hummingbird (*Selasphorus rufus*), strayed, once, to Big Diomede Island on the Siberian side of the Bering Strait. Wherever they first evolved, hummingbirds first flourished in the tropical lowlands of South America. From there, probably between six and twelve million years ago, a number of hummingbird lineages colonized the rising Andes. Here live some of a neotropical birder's most sought-after treasures: the Sword-billed Hummingbird (*Ensifera ensifera*), with a bill longer than its head and body combined, or the rare Marvellous Spatuletail (*Loddigesia mirabilis*) of Peru, whose male sports immense tail rackets that dance around the displaying bird like independent, attendant creatures.

Today the richest diversity of hummingbirds is to be found in tropical Andean countries: Colombia has around 150 species, Ecuador 140 and Peru 120. These countries owe this richness to the great range of Andean habitats found there — from lowland valleys to the alpine peaks that are home to the hillstars (*Oreotrochilus* spp.), and the Bearded Helmetcrest (*Oxypogon guerinii*) — and to a tendency for hummingbird populations to be marooned on isolated mountain clusters or separated by the Atlantic and Pacific slopes of the Andean chain. By contrast, Brazil, with its vast Amazonian lowlands, its extensive tropical savannas and the Atlantic Forest of its far southeast, boasts only 84 species.

As hummingbirds established themselves in the mountains, they evolved to meet the challenges of high altitude and alpine conditions. Hummingbirds at high elevations evolved stronger feet and longer, broader and blunter wings, better able to keep their owners aloft in increasingly thinner air. Many developed shorter, thinner bills better able to deal with the tiny, closely packed flowers of alpine composites (members of the daisy family). Only one major hummingbird lineage, the forest-dwelling hermits, fails to show these changes with altitude. Gary Stiles has suggested that this may explain why there are no hermits above about 6,600 feet (2,000 m), the upper limits of the heliconia flowers on which hermits largely depend.

Some hummingbird lineages pressed northwards, across the Isthmus of Darien. Over 100 species live today in Mexico and Central America. Some 58 species have been recorded in Mexico, a dozen of which are found nowhere else. Costa Rica, a far smaller country, boasts 54 and Panama has 59. Farther north, hummingbirds penetrated North America as far as Alaska and Newfoundland. Sixteen species breed regularly north of the Mexican border, though only eight reach any great distance beyond it: Rufous, Allen's (*S. sasin*), Broad-tailed (*S. platycercus*), Calliope (*S. calliope*), Anna's (*Calypte anna*), Costa's (*C. costae*), Black-chinned (*Archilochus alexandri*) and the sole breeding species in eastern North America, the Ruby-throated Hummingbird (*A. colubris*). The others stop at the Texas borderlands or the southern mountains of Arizona and New Mexico. One, the Buff-bellied Hummingbird (*Amazilia yucatanensis*), has been expanding its range eastward in coastal Texas. It could one day breed in Louisiana, where it shows up increasingly in winter.

In smaller numbers, hummingbirds spread southward into temperate South America, where the Green-backed Firecrown (*Sephanoides sephaniodes*), the most southerly of all, reaches Tierra del Fuego at the continent's tip. The Juan Fernandez Islands, 418 miles (672 km) over the Pacific from the coast of Chile, have a hummingbird of their own, the Critically Endangered Juan Fernandez Firecrown (*S. fernandensis*). Like high Andean hummingbirds, it has strong feet, perches to feed and visits mostly composites.

The West Indies (leaving aside Trinidad and Tobago, the Netherlands Antilles and the southwestern Caribbean islands of San Andrés and Providencia, which are, biologically speaking, detached bits of South America) are home to an array of hummingbirds whose ancestors must have reached the islands by crossing the open ocean. Of the 16 species breeding in the islands today, all but one, the Rufous-breasted Hermit (*Glaucis hirsutus*) of Grenada, are endemic (found nowhere else), although a few have strayed occasionally to North America. The Ruby-throated Hummingbird is a rare winter transient in the islands. The hermit, a widespread species in northern South America, probably arrived on Grenada fairly recently from either Trinidad or Tobago. Hermits from these three islands are genetically distinct from birds on the South American mainland. The endemic hummingbirds of the West Indies include the spectacular Red-billed Streamertail (*Trochilus polytmus*), national symbol of Jamaica, and the Bee Hummingbird (*Mellisuga helenae*) of Cuba, whose male, weighing only 1/20 of an ounce (1.6 g), is the smallest bird in the world.

A Bewildering Variety

There are over 340 living species of hummingbird (350 by one recent count). We are still discovering new ones: the Gorgeted Puffleg (*Eriocnemis isabellae*) was described only in 2007 (see p. 66) and the Black-capped Woodnymph (*Thalurania nigricapilla*, probably not a distinct species) in 2009. Only one other bird family, the 377-strong tanagers (Thraupidae), contains more species. This bewildering variety long frustrated ornithologists. Jimmy McGuire of the University of California, Berkeley, and his colleagues recently used genetic analyses to rearrange hummingbirds into what appear to be natural groups, or clades, each derived from a single common ancestor. These new studies confirm, as has long been thought, that the hummingbird family falls into two broad groups: the long-billed, dull-colored sicklebills and hermits (Phaethornithinae) and all the others (Trochilinae). One little group of four species, traditionally included in the Trochilinae, may have split from the main hummingbird line before the hermits did. The topazes are, with one exception, brilliantly iridescent birds, and if they really are relics of early hummingbird history, then the relatively drab hermits may have secondarily lost their bright colors as they took up life in the dim light of the forest interior.

The hummingbird family lineages, as we now understand them, are:

Topazes (Topazinae [or Florisugini], 4 species).
The male Crimson Topaz (*Topaza pella*) and its close cousin the Fiery Topaz (*T. pyra*) are spectacular ruby, gold and emerald hummingbirds, the largest in the family after the Giant Hummingbird (*Patagona gigas*). Two of their central tail feathers are prolonged into stiff streamers that curve inward, crossing over each other. Even the females are colorful for a hummingbird, emerald green with touches of the male's crimson and gold. Topazes are birds of the Amazonian rainforest, where they seek nectar in the crowns of flowering trees.

The White-necked Jacobin (*Florisuga mellivora*), its males crisply patterned in green, white and iridescent blue, ranges from Mexico to Amazonian Brazil. The Black Jacobin (*F. fusca*), found in coastal forests from southeastern Brazil to Argentina, is a duller bird. Both sexes are mostly black and white, touched on the back and wings with olive bronze. Birds of the canopy and forest edge, the White-necked can be found in coffee and cacao plantations, while the Black frequently visits Brazilian gardens.

Hermits (Phaethornithinae, 37 species).
Hermits, including sicklebills (*Eutoxeres* spp.) and barbthroats (*Threnetes* spp.), are largely confined to the inte-

White-necked Jacobin
(*Florisuga mellivora*)

rior of tropical forests, where they feed from the tubular flowers of heliconias and similar plants. Though some are quite large, others are among the smallest of hummingbirds. The sexes of most hermits differ little from each other. They are distinctive and easily recognizable birds, mostly rust, brown or gray in color. A few, in particular the White-whiskered Hermit (*Phaethornis yaruqui*) of northwestern South America, are mostly iridescent green. Typical hermits (*Phaethornis* spp. and *Anopetia* spp.) have graduated tails, elongated, white-tipped central tail feathers and long, curved bills. Other hermit bills range from the nearly straight beak of the Saw-billed Hermit (*Ramphodon naevius*) to the exaggeratedly decurved structures of the two sicklebills (*Eutoxeres* spp.).

Hermits differ from other hummingbirds in a number of ways, including their near-lack of iridescent colors, distinctive gaping displays and hanging nests, often suspended from the tip of a leaf. Most male hermits advertise for mates at communal display grounds called *leks*, a habit less common, though more widespread, than once thought in other hummingbirds (see p. 58).

"Typical" Hummingbirds (Trochilinae) are divided into seven groups:

Mangoes (Polytmini, 27 species).

The large, robust hummingbirds bearing the name "mango" (*Anthracothorax* spp.) include three species confined to the West Indies and another, the Green-breasted Mango (*A. prevostii*), that has strayed from its Middle American range as far as Wisconsin and North Carolina. Other members of the group include birds formerly placed on widely separated branches of the hummingbird family tree: violet-ears (*Colibri* spp.), lancebills (*Doryfera* spp.), caribs (*Eulampis* spp.), goldenthroats (*Polytmus* spp.), fairies (*Heliothryx* spp.), the Ruby-topaz Hummingbird (*Chrysolampis mosquitus*) and the tiny, nomadic Horned Sungem (*Heliactin bilopha*) of the grasslands and cerrado scrublands of Suriname, Brazil and Bolivia. The Tooth-billed Hummingbird (*Androdon aequatorialis*), of the Pacific slope from Panama to Ecuador, appears to belong with the mangoes, though it was long thought to be a sort of hermit. A few other hummingbirds probably fit here too.

Coquettes (Lesbiini, 60 species).

Coquettes (*Lophornis* spp.) are very small hummingbirds (though with rather strong feet) whose males are decorated with an array of crests and cheek frills. Their nearest relatives are the thorntails (*Discosura* spp.), including the Racket-tailed Coquette (*D. longicauda*).

The coquette lineage as we now understand it is a much broader assemblage, including at least 13 additional genera. The firecrowns (*Sephanoides*), the most southerly hummers of all, belong here. While *Lophornis* and *Discosura* species live mostly in tropical lowlands, the others are mountain birds. The Bearded Helmetcrest (*Oxypogon guerinii*) and the Ecuadorian Hillstar (*Oreotrochilus chimborazo*) live near the snowline, ranging up to 17,000 feet (5,200 m). Most of the rest are birds of mid- to high-mountain cloud forests and páramo in the northern and central Andes. They include the nine metaltails (*Metallura* spp.), the sylphs (*Aglaiocercus* spp.) and trainbearers (*Lesbia* spp.), with their extraordinarily long tails, and the shortest-billed of all hummingbirds, the Purple-backed Thornbill (*Ramphomicron microrhynchum*), whose scientific name means "short-bill short-bill."

Brilliants (Coeligenini, 48 species).

Brilliants and their close cousins the coquettes make up a larger group of related, mostly montane hummingbirds that has been dubbed the "Andean Clade." Brilliants, like many of the coquette group, are forest birds of the northern and central Andes. Among their 12 or 13 genera are some of the most striking birds in the family: coronets (*Boissonneaua* spp.), incas (*Coeligena* spp.), pufflegs (*Eriocnemis* spp.) and the brilliants themselves (*Heliodoxa* spp.), as well as the charming Booted Rackettail (*Ocreatus underwoodi*), the Great Sapphirewing (*Pterophanes cyanopterus*) — one of the few hummingbirds with iridescent wings — the extraordinary Sword-billed Hummingbird (*Ensifera ensifera*), and, apparently, the weird and wonderful Marvelous Spatuletail (*Loddigesia mirabilis*). Two Venezuelan hummingbirds, the Violet-breasted Hummingbird (*Sternoclyta cyanopectus*) and the endangered Scissor-tailed Hummingbird (*Hylonympha macrocerca*), are probably members of this group, and one lowland hummingbird, the Brazilian Ruby (*Clytolaema rubricauda*) of southeastern Brazil, is either an emerald or an isolated member of the brilliants.

Giant Hummingbird (Patagonini, 1 species).

At up to 8½ inches (22 cm) in length and weighing over ¾ ounce (20 g), the Giant is the largest of all hummingbirds. Its flight is distinctive and swift-like. When it hovers, its wings beat slowly enough to follow. Both sexes are rather plain, dull olive above with a white rump and either dull cinnamon (male) or grayish (female) below. The Giant is a fairly common bird of dry, open country and cactus-covered hillsides from southwestern Colombia south to northwestern Argentina and south-central Chile. Its most southerly populations migrate across the Andes in the austral autumn and winter.

Once thought to be only a large and rather odd-looking inca, the Giant Hummingbird does not fit obviously into any of the other groups. It may, though, be closest to mountain gems, bees and emeralds.

Mountain Gems (Lampornithini, 17 species).

Mountaingems (*Lampornis* spp.), starthroats (*Heliomaster* spp.) and the Fiery-throated Hummingbird (*Panterpe insignis*) of Costa Rica and western Panama form a small group of large hummingbirds, usually with brightly colored iridescent throats, found mostly in the mountain forests of Mexico and Central America. One of the most gorgeous birds in the family, the Garnet-throated Hummingbird (*Lamprolaima rhami*), is a locally common inhabitant of mountain forests from southern Mexico to Honduras. Three of the four starthroats are widespread in the lowlands of eastern South America (two are confined there). The most northerly of the mountain gems, the Blue-throated and Magnificent Hummingbirds (*Lampornis clemenciae* and *Eugenes fulgens*), cross the Mexican border into the southwestern United States. Their spectacular size (they are the largest hummingbirds to breed north of Mexico) makes them standout visitors to hummingbird feeders in the Chiricahua Mountains of southeastern Arizona. Another mountain gem, the Plain-capped Starthroat (*Heliomaster constantii*), occasionally wanders north into southeastern Arizona at the end of its nesting season.

Bees (Mellisugini, 36 species).

This group takes its name from the minute Bee Hummingbird (*Mellisuga helenae*) of Cuba. Its members might better be called woodstars, the name used for a number of tropical bees including the Bahama Woodstar (*Calliphlox evelynae*), a West Indian species that has strayed to southern Florida.

These are the hummingbirds that are most familiar to birders in the United States, and the only ones regularly found in Canada. All the hummingbirds that breed any distance north and east of the Rio Grande or the southwest border mountains of the United States are bees, including the Ruby-throated Hummingbird (*Archilochus colubris*), the only breeding hummingbird of eastern North America, and the Rufous Hummingbird (*Selasphorus rufus*), which nests as far north as Alaska. Male bees court their females with spectacular aerial dive displays (see p. 59). Like their closest relatives the much larger mountain gems, they usually confine their brightest and most iridescent colors to a brilliant throat patch, or gorget, whose feathers can be fluffed out, when necessary, into a glittering puff or fan. Males of the sheartails (*Tilmatura* spp. and *Doricha* spp.), and the Sparkling-tailed Woodstar (*Tilmatura dupontii*), of Mexico and northern Central America, add elongated tail-feathers, strikingly barred black and white in the woodstar and white with black tips in the Peruvian Sheartail (*Thaumastura cora*).

Emeralds (Trochilini, 108 species).

This largest of hummingbird lineages (the genus *Amazilia* alone contains 30 species) includes many of the commonest and most familiar tropical hummingbirds. Only a few cross the Mexican border. The Buff-bellied Hummingbird (*A. yucatanensis*) is established and spreading in southern Texas, and it may winter as far east as western Florida. The Broad-billed Hummingbird (*Cynanthus latirostris*), whose rich greens and blues make the male the most "tropical-looking" of U.S. hummingbirds, is a feature of southwestern canyons, where lucky birders may also come across the equally handsome White-eared and Violet-crowned Hummingbirds (*Hylocharis leucotis* and *Amazilia violiceps*).

Emeralds come in all shapes and sizes, from the large sabrewings (*Campylopterus* spp.) to the Snowcap (*Microchera albocoronata*), a diminutive, purple-and-white favorite of visiting birders in Costa Rica. Woodnymphs (*Thalurania* spp.) and sapphires (*Chlorestes* spp. and *Chrysuronia* spp.) are brilliantly iridescent, but the Sombre Hummingbird (*Aphantochroa cirrochloris*) of eastern Brazil is one of the plainest of the family. A few species add ornamental feathers: the crest of the Antillean Crested Hummingbird (*Orthorhyncus cristatus*) of the West Indies and the much more extensive head plume of the Plovercrest (*Stephanoxis lalandi*) of southeastern Brazil; the long, deeply forked tail of the Swallow-tailed Hummingbird (*Eupetomena macroura*), and especially the crest and extensive, wave-edged tail streamers of the two streamertails (*Trochilus* spp.) of Jamaica. Nineteenth-century naturalist Philip Henry Gosse hailed the Red-billed Streamertail (*T. polytmus*) as "the gem of Jamaican ornithology," whose "slender form, velvet crest, emerald bosom, and lengthened tail-plumes, render it one of the most elegant even of this most brilliant family."

Violet Sabrewing (*Campylopterus hemileucurus*)

THREE

How Hummingbirds Fly

Hummingbirds are not the only birds that hover. Sunbirds can and do hover in front of flowers, at least briefly. Birds of prey such as the American Kestrel (*Falco sparverius*) and White-tailed Kite (*Elanus leucurus*) hover over open fields as part of their hunting technique. Hummingbirds are not even the only birds that fly backward. Tropicbirds (Phaethontidae), tropical seabirds quite unlike hummingbirds, do that as part of their aerial displays.

However, no other birds are as proficient as hummingbirds at aerial maneuvering, and no others are so utterly dependent on it. Hummingbirds are the only birds that can maintain steady, controlled hovering over long periods of time. A hummingbird can even hover in heavy rain without losing control — quite a feat for such a tiny creature. Its ability to hang, motionless and steady, in the air — a physically difficult and energetically costly thing to do — is based on special modifications of its flight mechanism, and on an ability to burn oxygen at a rate that is the highest, relative to its body size, of any vertebrate.

Hummingbird wings differ markedly from the wings of other birds. Both swifts and hummingbirds have extremely short upper arms and very long hands. Most of the wing area of a hummingbird — some 75 percent, more than in any other bird — is made up of the primaries, the feathers sprouting from the bones of its wrist and hand. This makes hummingbird wings particularly stiff, so that a flying hummer can look more like an insect than a bird.

Active bird flight (as opposed to soaring or gliding) requires a powered downstroke. Most birds follow this with a weaker upstroke that rotates and lifts the wings into position for the next downward flap. That works for the short bursts of hovering most other birds can manage, but key to the ability to hover like a hummingbird is a need to deliver an upstroke that is nearly as powerful as the downstroke. The muscle that powers the hummingbird upstroke, the supracoracoideus, is relatively larger (in comparison with the pectoralis major, the chief muscle that drives the downstroke) than in any other bird family.

A bird's wing, however, is not symmetrical. In normal flight, its concave lower surface delivers thrust on the downstroke, and its convex upper surface reduces drag as the bird lifts its wings for the next beat.

Hovering hummingbirds stay in place by rotating their wings to deliver a powered upstroke. A Rufous Hummingbird (*Selasphorus rufus*) may do this 55 times in a single second.

Hummingbirds can use the upstroke to deliver about 25 percent of their hovering power by supinating, rotating the bones in the arm and hand so that the lower surface faces upwards (hovering insects do much the same thing). As the bird flips its wing over and back again, its wing tip describes a figure eight in the air (try this with your hand to get the idea). Most of the rotation happens in the wrist, and since most of its wing area arises from its hand a twist of the wrist affects a greater proportion of a hummingbird's flight surface than it would in other birds.

Both upstroke and downstroke have to happen quickly enough to keep the bird stable in mid-air. Rufous Hummingbirds (*Selasphorus rufus*) have been recorded beating their wings 55 times per second. They need rapid wingbeats not just for stability, but because they are so very small. The aerodynamic force that a flapping wing generates depends on its area and flapping speed. The smaller the bird, the smaller (in general) the wing area, so the faster it has to flap to stay aloft. This is true even within hummingbirds: larger, longer-winged hummingbirds flap their wings more slowly than smaller species, and the wing beats of the largest of all, the Giant Hummingbird (*Patagona gigas*), can be slow enough to follow with the eye.

To stay in place without straining its flight muscles, a hummingbird has to get the deepest possible wingbeats (not to mention other, more subtle, wing movements) out of the least muscle activity. That is especially true at higher elevations, where the air is thin and flight more demanding. The higher up they live, the more deeply the many hummingbirds that live in the Andes beat their wings to compensate. Technically, hummingbirds need a high muscle-to-wing transmission ratio, and thanks to the way their wing bones are structured they have one.

The key is the humerus, the bone of the upper arm. Tyson Hendrick and his co-workers recently confirmed that, in hummingbirds, the humerus forms part of an energy-saving gear mechanism. In most birds, the humerus is a long bone that points outward, away from the body, in flight. To produce a deep wing beat, the humerus pivots up and down. That takes a fair bit of muscular effort. A hummingbird, though, has the shortest humerus for its body size of any bird. Instead of pointing outward, it is directed backward, almost at right angles to the leading edge of the wing. During the flight stroke, instead of swinging up and down it spins around its long axis, aided by a particularly mobile shoulder joint. This sweeps the wing up and down rather in the way that the axis of a helicopter rotor spins its blades, except of course that the humerus must rotate back and forth rather than turning in continuous circles. Rotation reaches its peak speed in the middle of the wing beat, when the wing tip is also moving at its fastest, adding power to both the upstroke and the downstroke without a great deal of additional strain. The result is a deep wing beat delivered with much less muscular effort than other birds need to accomplish the same thing.

When a hummingbird flies backward, it tilts its body towards the vertical and bends its head forward to keep its bill horizontal for feeding. Since it is now more upright than usual, the bird has to swivel its wings

HUMMINGBIRD

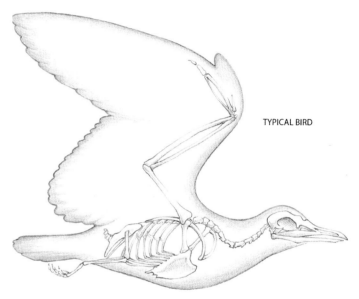

TYPICAL BIRD

forward so that they still beat downward as well as backward. Using wind-tunnel experiments on Anna's Hummingbirds (*Calypte anna*), Nir Sapir and Robert Dudley have found that, despite these postural changes, flying backward costs a hummingbird no more than flying forwards, and rather less than does hovering. It probably costs the bird less energy than it would need to turn around in mid-air to back away from a flower — which may explain why hummingbirds developed their backward flying skills in the first place.

The hummingbird skeleton (above left) has evolved for a life on the wing. Compared to the skeleton of a typical bird (above), its greatly shortened arm bones support a stiffened wing for hovering and insect-like flight, and an expanded keel on the sternum, or breastbone, provides added space for the attachment of powerful flight muscles.

FOUR

How Hummingbirds Refuel

A Need for Sugar

The inextricable bond between hummingbirds and flowers has driven the evolution of both bird and plant. Nectar is not their only food, but for much of their lives most hummingbirds are utterly dependent on the sugars nectar provides.

The sugar a flower produces has its own reason for being there. Nectar is a bait to lure in pollinators. Floral nectars may contain sucrose, a complex sugar, or simple sugars such as glucose and fructose. Different pollinators may prefer one or the other. Though some nectar-feeding songbirds lack the enzyme that breaks down sucrose and will starve on a diet of it, hummingbirds are able to digest sucrose molecules. Hummers usually prefer flowers that produce them, especially if they are highly concentrated in the flower's nectar. Wild Green-backed Firecrowns (*Sephanoides sephaniodes*) in the temperate forests of southern Chile have been shown to prefer (as most hummingbirds probably do) sucrose over glucose and fructose, and (probably as a consequence, though this is not certain) sucrose is the chief sugar in the nectar of 11 species of flowering plants that Firecrowns pollinate.

Hummingbirds may prefer simpler sugars if a flower's sucrose offering is too dilute. Their tongues probably have separate taste receptors for each sugar. In a series of tests, Broad-billed Hummingbirds (*Cynanthus latirostris*) seemed able to detect, and taste, fructose at lower concentrations than for either sucrose or glucose. They preferred dilute fructose solutions to dilute solutions of other sugars that they may not have been able to taste — a sign that hummingbirds do, indeed, have a sweet tooth. Binging on dilute, but tasty, sugar may not be a very good strategy. Sucrose concentrations may vary, from flower to flower, from as little as seven to as much as 60 percent. In temperate Chile, Paulina González-Gómez found that over the course of a day, nectar in flowers visited by Green-backed Firecrowns varied by more than nine times in sucrose concentration and by more than 300 times in overall quantity. The ideal concentration, as far as a hummingbird is concerned, may depend not on sweetness but on such things as the amount of liquid it has to drink, and carry around in its stomach, to get the sugar it needs (hummingbirds turn over more body water per day than any other vertebrate). To pick, and consume, the best and

Coppery-headed Emerald
(*Elvira cupreiceps*)

most efficient meal, a hummingbird needs both to detect sugar concentration, and to tell when it has had enough. When experimenters presented Rufous Hummingbirds (*Selasphorus rufus*) with a sucrose concentration different from the one they had been drinking, the birds did not change they amount they drank right away (as they might have done if they were going by taste alone), but adjusted their meal size over the course of a few visits. It was as though they needed time for their bodies to give them physiological feedback about the effect that their new meals were having.

If flowers are scarce, hummingbirds may turn to other sources for their sugar supply. Hummingbirds have been seen feeding on juices spilling from fruits, sugar-rich liquids oozing from lesions on diseased scrub oak trees, and the sweet honeydew excreted by some scale insects. They have been recorded defending trees infested with scale insects against rivals, and even against large wasps. Today, they may rely on human beings and artificial feeders, but other birds have been creating hummingbird feeders since long before we came on the scene.

Sapsuckers (*Sphyrapicus* spp.) are North American woodpeckers that systematically chisel rows of shallow sap wells in the bark of living trees. Hummingbirds follow sapsuckers around, feeding on the sap that seeps into the wells or snapping up tiny insects that the wells attract (some tropical mountain hummingbirds follow Acorn Woodpeckers [*Melanerpes formicivorus*] for the same reason). In early spring, sapsucker wells may provide returning hummingbirds with a valuable source of food before many flowers are available. The activities of Yellow-bellied Sapsuckers (*S. varius*) in the north woods may allow Ruby-throated Hummingbirds (*Archilochus colubris*) to arrive on their breeding grounds earlier, and to stay there longer, than they would if they had to depend on flowers alone.

Flowers and Brains

Hummingbirds must find hundreds of flowers every day, as rapidly and efficiently as possible. Amazilia Hummingbirds (*Amazilia amazilia*) may visit more than 30 flowers a minute. A feeding hummingbird has to know what kinds of flowers have the most sucrose-rich nectar, where they are, and when they are at their peak of nectar production. It has to know how long to wait before a flower it has already fed from is worth revisiting. In short, a hummingbird needs phenomenal spatial and temporal memory, coupled with a searchable, updatable database of flower types, flower development and nectar production. It needs an on-board computer, one capable of learning and processing new information, and it needs to pack it into a brain the size of a pea.

The need to find the right kind of food has made hummingbird brains unique. They may be small, but their hippocampal region, the part of the brain believed to be associated with spatial memory, is enormous — two to five times larger, in proportion to overall forebrain size, than in any other bird studied, including birds that store food (such as seeds) and need good spatial memory to find it again. The hippocampal volume of a Long-billed Hermit (*Phaethornis longirostris*) is almost 10 times larger than that of an American Redstart (*Setophaga ruticilla*), a songbird that outweighs the hermit by only a few grams.

How does a hummingbird use its highly developed brain to find the right flowers? There are two main ways to find an object: beaconing — knowing what the object looks like and homing in when you see it — and spatial recognition — remembering where the object is, perhaps with the help of surrounding landmarks, and heading for that spot whether you can see what you are looking for or not. Studies by Ileana Nuri Flores-Abreu, Andrew Hurly and Susan Healy have shown that wild Rufous Hummingbirds (*Selasphorus rufus*) can learn the location of a productive flower after a single visit. To see if this was spatial recognition, the experimenters moved their test flowers to a spot that was 6½ feet (2 m) away, but still in plain sight. If the birds were beaconing, they should have flown straight for the flower in its new position as soon as they could see it. Instead, when they came back after about 15 minutes, they first flew to the spot where the flower had been. Eventually the birds did learn to fly directly to the flower itself — a switch from spatial recognition to beaconing that may have involved switching the finding process to another part of their brains.

If hummingbirds really do store the location of every single flower they visit, it would be an unparalleled feat of memory. They're not perfect at it, though. In another set of experiments, Flores-Abreu's team found that if the hummingbirds had to select which flower among a group of test flowers they had already visited had a nectar reward, they had trouble picking the right spot if the flowers were too close together. At 12 inches (30 cm) apart the birds could home on the right flower without trouble, but at 2 inches (5 cm) they were likely to make mistakes. They were also better at discriminating among flowers spaced horizontally than if the experimenters arranged them vertically. That may be where beaconing comes in. Guillermo Perez and his co-workers showed that while White-eared Hummingbirds (*Hylocharis leucotis*) in Mexico use their locating ability to revisit *Penstemon* spp. plants, they may rely on visual cues when choosing among flowers on the same plant.

Hummingbirds appear able to calculate how long it will take for an empty flower to restore its nectar supply, and to time their visits accordingly. Researchers presenting wild Rufous Hummingbirds with artificial flowers refilled at 10- and 20-minute intervals found that the birds adjusted to the refill schedule and visited the ten-minute flowers more frequently than the 20-minute flowers. They were also able to remember which flowers they had recently visited and emptied. Paulina González-Gómez and her colleagues found that Green-backed Firecrowns (*Sephanoides sephaniodes*) appear to be better at the necessary calculations for flowers that replenish themselves quickly. The birds may even prefer to visit flowers with lower-quality nectar that refill at a high, easily predictable rate to richer flowers that are slower, and perhaps less regular, in rebuilding their supplies. That may reflect more than a limitation of memory: though higher-yield flowers may supply richer rewards, they may take more energy to defend against other birds eager to get their share. When it comes to energy, hummingbirds appear to be cautious investors.

How Hummingbirds Feed

Watching a hummingbird dip its tongue into a flower, it is easy to suppose that it is sucking up nectar in the same way that we sip through a straw. Drinking through a straw, though, requires us to use our mouths to create suction. It needs lips and cheeks, things birds don't have. We mammals probably evolved the ability to suck in connection with nursing, and birds don't do that either.

So, if a hummingbird can't suck — at least, not in the way we do — how does it get nectar into its mouth? Scientists have wondered about this for some time. Philip Henry Gosse admitted in 1847 that "I do not thoroughly understand the mode by which liquids are taken up by a Humming-bird's tongue, though I have carefully watched the process." Recent studies using high-speed videography and analyses of fluid dynamics may, unexpectedly, have given us not just one solution to Gosse's mystery, but two.

The business end of a hummingbird's tongue is split in two, each half tipped with a fringe of tiny structures called lamellae. Each side of the split tongue tends to roll into a tube when wet — really a narrow groove, as the tube remains open at the edges. Ornithologists have long assumed that hummingbirds draw nectar into these grooves by capillary attraction, the same process

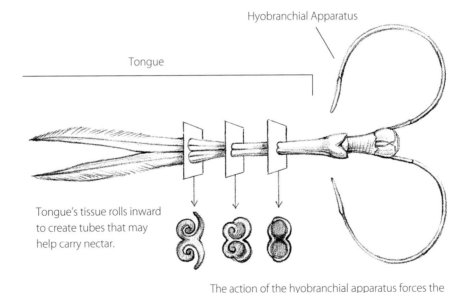

Hyobranchial Apparatus

Tongue

Tongue's tissue rolls inward to create tubes that may help carry nectar.

The tip of a hummingbird's tongue is split into two parts, each fringed with tiny projections, or lamellae. The tongue sits on the hyobranchial apparatus, which slides forward when the bird inserts its tongue into a flower. Scientists still debate about how the bird's tongue draws nectar into its mouth.

The action of the hyobranchial apparatus forces the hummingbird's tongue beyond its bill. The forked tip picks up nectar, but the tongue is not designed for catching insects as was once believed.

that allows you to soak up water with a paper towel. You may have demonstrated capillary attraction yourself in science class, using a thin glass tube. When a hummingbird dips the tip of its tongue into a flower's nectar reserve, the nectar should flow up the grooves without the bird having to do anything further.

The problem is that detailed measurements show that the rate at which a hummingbird takes up nectar does not match what you would predict if the only thing happening was passive capillary attraction. Something else must be going on.

A hummingbird's tongue, unlike your science teacher's glass capillary tube, is neither closed nor inflexible. Its shape can be changed: it can bend, spread open or close over itself. The hummingbird can't make these changes by itself. Bird tongues lack the internal nerves and musculature that you use to stick out, wiggle or twist your own tongue. Instead, their tongue muscles attach to the skeletal structure on which the tongue sits — the hyo-branchial apparatus — and act by sliding the supporting bones back and forth along the bird's skull. In effect, all a hummingbird can do is stick its tongue out of its mouth and pull it back in again. How much it can do so depends on the length of the bones in the tongue's skeletal support. Hummingbirds have long supporting bones that wrap around the skull, and have lost the muscles that, in other birds, attach the tongue's bones to the vocal apparatus. Without these muscles holding the bones back, hummingbirds can stick out their tongues farther than most other birds.

Once a hummingbird's tongue enters a flower, any changes in its shape are caused not by the bird but either by collisions with the flower itself, or by contact with the nectar the flower holds. If these changes improve its ability to draw up nectar, the bird gains a better meal without having to expend extra energy in the process.

So what kinds of changes are we talking about, and what effect might they have? This is where the two explanations differ.

One, favored by Wonjung Kim of MIT and his colleagues, is that as capillary attraction pulls nectar into the tongue grooves, the surface tension of the liquid draws the flexible edges of the tongue together — a process they refer to, delightfully, as capillary origami. The tongue becomes even more tubular than before, and, Kim argues, the new shape increases the rate at which nectar flows along it. Kim calls the hummingbird's tongue a "self-assembling capillary syphon." Kim's studies may also explain why hummingbirds seem to prefer flowers with a lower sugar concentration than do, say, bees. Highly concentrated nectar, though it has more food value per drop, is just too viscous (or syrupy) to take up by capillary attraction. Most bees (the insects, not the hummingbirds) simply lap up sticky nectar with their tongues.

Alejandro Rico-Guevara and Margaret Rubega of the University of Connecticut argue instead that capillary attraction has little to do with nectar-feeding. Instead, the tongue acts as a fluid trap. Before the tip of the tongue enters a liquid it is already wet, the two sides are stuck together and the lamellae are tightly furled up. As soon as the tip enters a liquid it unfurls and the lamellae spread out, only to draw together again when the bird withdraws. Every time this happens the tongue traps a small amount of liquid. Rico and Rubega found that trapping happens even with the isolated tongues of dead hummingbirds, proving that the process is entirely passive. Fluid trapping may not only be faster than capillary attraction, depending on how quickly a hummingbird extends and withdraws its tongue (and that can be very quick indeed — the whole cycle can take as little as $\frac{1}{20}$th of a second), but it can work when only a thin film of nectar is left inside a flower.

Fluid trapping may explain how a hummingbird gets liquid onto the part of the tongue that is actually below the surface of a flower's pool of nectar. How, though, does nectar travel up the rest of it? The journey may be relatively long, depending on the length of the hummingbird's bill and tongue, the shape of the flower, the amount of nectar it holds (or has left after the bird has been drinking for a time), and how far down the floral tube the bird has to stick its tongue to get the nectar. Kim argues that, at this point, capillary attraction — aided by origami — takes over.

Rico and Rubega, though, have two problems with this idea. First, it appears that capillary origami, rather than speeding up the movement of nectar, actually slows it down. Second, when a hummingbird squeezes nectar out of its tongue with its bill, it flattens the grooves in the tongue — and they stay flattened until the bird sticks its tongue into the nectar again. That means that the capillary tubes that are supposed to transfer nectar up the tongue are no longer there. How, then, does the nectar get up the tongue? Rico and Rubega have found that when the tongue tip enters the nectar, a wave of fluid starts to move upwards, opening and filling the grooves as it goes.

This is not capillary attraction — the fluid moves far too quickly for that — but exactly how this new mechanism works we do not fully understand.

We also don't quite understand how nectar trapped at the tip of a hummingbird's tongue, or loaded in its grooves, makes its way down the bird's throat. We now know the bird uses structures in its bill, including fine serrations along the bill edge, to strip nectar from its tongue (this is what a hummingbird may be doing when it continues to flick its tongue in and out even after it withdraws from a flower), but we are still working out the details of how it is done.

To get enough sugar from a nectar diet dilute enough to flow along their tongues, hummingbirds take on a tremendous amount of water — up to seven times their body mass per day, a figure more like that of a fish or a frog than a bird. They have to get rid of most of it as quickly as possible. When they are not feeding, they face the opposite problem. Bird kidneys do not operate the way ours do. They cannot produce a concentrated urine, and hummingbirds risk dehydrating as they eliminate their body wastes. In fact, they do dehydrate to some degree. They lose water by evaporation at a rate of about two percent of their body weight per hour for a resting hummingbird. At night, or during long flights, hummingbirds need to save water, not get rid of it.

To get around these problems, hummingbirds still depend on their kidneys. Like other birds, they are able to change the rate at which their kidneys filter their body fluids. Though the rate rises during the day, it does not seem to rise quickly enough to get rid of their excess water. Instead, as hummingbirds take on more water, they reduce the amount their bodies reabsorb after their kidneys have filtered it. Sunbirds and honeyeaters, by the way, can do this too. Bradley Hartmann Bakken, Paolo Saba and their colleagues have demonstrated that Broad-tailed Hummingbirds (*Selasphorus platycercus*) and Green-backed Firecrowns (*Sephanoides sephaniodes*) cut down water loss at night by completely, or almost completely, shutting off their kidneys' filtration system, something other birds only seem able to do over a period of days. We are still not sure how they do it.

What Makes a Good Flower

Flowers that have evolved in partnership with hummingbirds share a number of features. From the plant's point of view, the most important may be the positions of the anthers, the organs that bear its pollen, and the style, the tube at the top of the ovary where pollen (preferably from another plant) must be deposited if the flower is to be fertilized. In many hummingbird flowers, the anthers are placed so that when a hummingbird inserts its bill for a nectar meal it gets a dab of pollen on its forehead (see p. 244), and the styles are placed so that when it visits another flower the pollen rubs off again onto the style.

The ideal hummingbird flower should be easy for the bird to reach, hard for other pollinators to get at and colored, shaped and placed either to attract a hummingbird's eye or to deter visitors that might carry its pollen to the wrong plant. In some plants, even nearby leaves are marked with bright color to draw the birds' attention. Hummingbird flowers are often tubular, ideal for penetration by a long-billed hummingbird but beyond reach

for most other birds. Their nectar tends to be dilute, the better to be taken up by a hummingbird's tongue. They may have little or no fragrance since hummingbirds, like most other birds, have a poor sense of smell.

Many hummingbird flowers hang downward. This keeps their nectar from being washed away in the rain, but hummingbirds that feed from such flowers do so at some cost. Nir Sapir and Robert Dudley recently demonstrated that hovering in the upright, head-up position Anna's Hummingbirds (*Calypte anna*) must use to take nectar from a vertically hanging flower costs them some 10 percent more metabolic effort than they need to reach a horizontal blossom. This may be why Green-backed Firecrowns (*Sephanoides sephaniodes*) seem to prefer horizontal mistletoe flowers to vertically hanging ones, though Ruby-throated Hummingbirds (*Archilochus colubris*), faced with a similar choice, apparently show no such preference. Hummingbirds that specialize on hanging flowers, such as the Sword-billed

Western Emerald
(*Chlorostilbon melanorhynchus*)

Hummingbird (*Ensifera ensifera*), have slightly upturned bills to make the job easier.

Hummingbird flowers are often red — not, perhaps, to attract hummingbirds, but to avoid attracting insects. Insects see red poorly, and may pass by a flower that a hummingbird is likely to visit. Hummingbirds probably do not have a fixed instinctive preference for red, though Robert Gegear and James Burns found that when Broad-tailed and Rufous Hummingbirds (*Selasphorus platycercus* and *S. rufus*) were tested on artificial flowers at the Rocky Mountain Biological Laboratory in Crested Butte, Colorado, they showed a strong preference for red over blue. Hummingbirds on their breeding grounds may pay little attention to color when deciding which flowers to visit, though color information may help them learn more quickly where the best flowers are. Red flowers seem particularly likely to be visited by migrating hummingbirds in places like California. A migrating hummingbird, passing briefly through unfamiliar territory, may not have the location information it uses to find flowers on its home turf. It may be drawn to the most conspicuous flowers that it sees, and red, as a color, stands out.

A flower that tries to reserve its nectar for its preferred pollinators risks being robbed. A bird with a bill too short to reach down a long floral tube can steal nectar by tearing through the flower from the outside, bypassing its pollen in the process. A number of birds indulge in such "nectar robbery." Flowerpiercers (*Diglossa* spp.), a group of tropical American songbirds, specialize in it, stealing nectar with hooked bill-tips that punch tiny holes in the bases of tubular flowers.

Short-billed hummingbirds can be nectar robbers too. In southeastern Brazil the *mulungu-do-litoral* tree (*Erythrina speciosa*) is pollinated by long-billed hummingbirds, but short-billed Gilded Sapphires (*Hylocharis chrysura*), Sapphire-spangled Emeralds (*Amazilia lactea*), and Swallow-tailed Hummingbirds (*Eupetomena macroura*) steal nectar by probing between the bases of its petals.

Fairies (*Heliothryx* spp.) are habitual nectar robbers. Alexander Skutch, a pioneer of tropical ornithology and a devotee of hummingbirds, called the Purple-crowned Fairy (*H. barroti*) an "incorrigible thief" that pierces the base of flowers with an "exceptionally sharp" bill "simply by pressing against them while hovering." Skutch noted that bypassing restrictions on legitimate pollinators gives the robbers a much wider choice of flowers.

Some nectar robbers actually use hummingbirds to get their meals. Hummingbird flower mites (Ascidae) feed on pollen and nectar from many hummingbird-pollinated flowers. To get from one flower to another, the mites climb onto the bill of a visiting hummingbird and hitch a ride in its nostrils (see p. 17). The mites, despite their size, provide the birds with serious competition. Carlos Lara and Juan Francisco Ornelas have demonstrated that mites reduce the nectar supplies in the Central American forest plant *Moussonia deppeana*, a relative of African violets, by up to 50 percent.

Oddly enough, some nectar robbers may help the plant. By reducing the amount of nectar available they may force pollinators to visit more flowers, increasing the chance that they will transfer pollen from one plant to another. That seems to be the case for the flower mites and *M. deppeana*. Experiments by Lara and Ornelas suggest that plants infested by mites may get more visits from Amethyst-throated Hummingbirds (*Lampornis amethystinus*), and set more seeds as a result. Not all robbers are this helpful: Austral Blackbirds (*Curaeus curaeus*) in Chile, robbing bromeliad blossoms pollinated by Giant Hummingbirds (*Patagona gigas*), often destroy the flowers altogether.

One long-flowered Andean plant, *Aphelandra runcinata*, has evolved a mechanism that allows short-billed hummingbirds to reach its nectar without having to rob it. Only a few hummingbirds have bills long enough to probe its blooms, but when a short-billed hummingbird pushes its head into one of its flowers the floral tube folds up like an accordion, allowing the bird to reach the nectar at its base and pollinate the flower in the process.

The right flower for feeding may depend not just on which species of hummingbird we are talking about, but which sex. In many hummingbirds, females have longer bills than males. In hermits the male tends to have the longer bill, but female bills tend to be more strongly curved, particularly in long-billed species like the Green Hermit (*Phaethornis guy*). Longer or more strongly curved bills may allow females to avoid having to deal with aggressive males by visiting flowers whose nectar the males cannot reach. Longer bills allow hummingbirds access to a wider range of flowers. Birds with curved bills can probe similarly curved flowers that straighter-billed birds have difficulty with.

The Purple-throated Carib (*Eulampis jugularis*) lives on islands in the eastern Caribbean. Both sexes have the same richly colored plumage, but their differences in size and bill shape are among the most extreme in hummingbirds. Male caribs are one-quarter larger than females, but the bills of females are 30 percent longer than the bills of males, and twice as strongly curved. The contrast is probably so great because caribs live on islands where there are few other hummingbird competitors. They may, as a result, have more environmental "space" to diverge from one another — a phenomenon known a "ecological release."

Purple-throated Caribs are the only pollinators of two species of *Heliconia*. On St. Lucia, one has long, curved flowers emerging from showy green bracts. It is visited by females, whose bills are significantly longer and more curved than in males. The other, which has red bracts and short, straight flowers, and is preferred by males. If the species that males prefer is rare, a form of the other species, with shorter flowers and red-and-green bracts, takes its place. On Dominica, the reverse happens: it is the species males prefer that has a second form, with yellow bracts and curved flowers that match the bills of females. Ethan Temeles and John Kress found that plants visited by females have fewer flowers, and therefore produce less nectar, than those defended by males. This is a good match between bird and plant, because male caribs are larger and more aggressive than females and require more energy in their diet. From the bird's point of view, these differences may allow the sexes to feed without getting in each other's way, and from the plant's, being visited by only one sex, and therefore by fewer birds, increases the chances that the hummingbirds will carry their pollen to the right flower.

It is, nonetheless, surprisingly rare to find an ecological "arrangement" between a hummingbird with a specialized bill and a plant with flowers that few other hummingbirds can reach. The best example is probably between the Sword-billed Hummingbird, a bird with a bill so long that other hummingbirds may try (at least in captivity) to use it as a perch, and *Passiflora mixta*, a passionflower with a narrow, extremely lengthy floral tube. The Sword-bills feed on a variety of long-tubed flowers, but so dependent is the plant on the bird for the spread of its pollen that in areas of the Andes where the forest has been cleared and the Sword-bills have disappeared, the plant may be following them into local extinction.

Hummingbirds and Insects

Nectar is a great source of energy, and being able to use it has surely been the key to hummingbird success. It isn't enough, though, for a complete diet. Nectar is very low in essential amino acids, the building blocks of the proteins the birds need to build muscles and grow feathers. To get amino acids, hummingbirds turn to another source: insects. Insects (and other small arthropods such as spiders) make up about a 10th, by mass, of a hummingbird's daily diet, and for some hummingbirds (particularly nesting females) even more. According to Gregor Yanega, a hummingbird needs the equivalent of about 300 fruit flies a day to survive. One captive Gilded Sapphire (*Hylocharis chrysura*) ate 677 fruit flies over the course of a 16-hour day. The number of insects a wild hummingbird

eats can vary. Wintering hummingbirds in a thorn forest in western Mexico spent almost all their foraging time on arrival hunting for insects, and almost two-thirds of their time just before departure, but spent hardly any time looking for insects in midwinter.

The need for arthropods in their diet may be particularly great when hummingbirds are breeding, and during their molting period, when birds shed old, worn feathers and grow a new set. Hummingbirds normally begin to molt once a year, after the breeding season. The molt season lasts about four to five months, though birds with access to rich food supplies may molt more quickly. At El Jaguar in the mountains of Nicaragua, Long-billed Hermits (*Phaethornis longirostris)* and Violet Sabrewings (*Campylopterus hemileucurus*) step up their consumption of arthropods during the breeding and molting seasons.

Hummingbirds can get some of their energy supply from the fats and proteins in insect bodies, especially when nectar supplies are low. In the Chiricahua Mountains of southeastern Arizona, the Magnificent Hummingbird (*Eugenes fulgens*) may get so much of its energy from insects and spiders (including small wasps and leafhoppers) that it may be able to get along, at least for a time, without resorting to flowers at all. Concentrating on arthropods may also help it avoid competing with other hummingbirds, including the more aggressive Blue-throated (*Lampornis clemenciae*), for access to flowers (or the artificial feeders that attract birders to the mountain resorts). Flowers can be scarce in the Chiricahuas before the monsoon rains. It may be that several of the hummingbird species that live there, including the Magnificent — and, perhaps, humming-birds in other places where nectar supplies are uncertain — turn to arthropods to get them through the lean times when nectar can be hard to come by.

Plenty of birds eat insects, but hummingbirds, as in so much of what they do, have their own way of going about it. It used to be thought that a hummingbird trapped tiny insects in the course of lapping up nectar, sweeping them from the flower with the tip of its tongue as it drank. Hummingbirds do pick up pollen, another source of amino acids, in that way (though they usually cannot digest it — oddly, hummingbirds have also been seen licking painted walls and road surfaces, probably in search of mineral salts), but it appears that they do not, or cannot, gather insects from flowers. Instead, hermits take them from plants or spider webs. Hermits (and other curve-billed hummingbirds) take a lot of spiders too, snatching them from their webs or pursuing them downwards if they try to escape on a strand of silk. In Costa Rica, the huge webs of Giant Orb-weaving Spiders (*Nephila clavipes*) make particularly attractive larders for Long-billed Hermits. A hermit relative, the Band-tailed Barbthroat (*Threnetes ruckeri*), specializes instead in hunting for jumping spiders in the forest undergrowth.

Other hummingbirds catch most of their insects in flight, though they will, to varying degrees, take insect prey while sitting on a perch. The idea of a hummingbird as a flycatcher seems counter-intuitive; the long, narrow beak of a hummingbird would seem to be exactly the wrong tool for snapping up a flying insect (compared to,

Magnificent Hummingbird (*Eugenes fulgens*)

Bronzy Inca (*Coeligena coeligena*)

Hummingbirds normally do not catch insects with the bill tip, but sweep them in at the gape. A hermit may pick an insect from a leaf with the tip of its bill, but to swallow its prey the bird tosses its catch in the air and flies at it, or backs up under it, catching the insect again in the back of its mouth. Gregor Yanega and Margaret Rubega used high-speed videography to show that as a hummingbird flies at an insect with open jaws, the lower mandible bows outward, and flexes downward by some 25 degrees. This widens its gape, increasing the chance that the bird will connect with its prey. The process is under precise muscular control, and it takes more energy to operate than the traps of broad-billed insect-catchers. Hummingbird bills, like those of many birds, are fairly flexible (otherwise, they might snap off in a fight or an accident), but as far as we know, no other bird — indeed, no other vertebrate — has a lower jaw that can bend in exactly this way.

Besides broadening the bird's gape, the flexion of a hummingbird's lower jaw sets up a trap that can spring shut with remarkable speed. Once the bill flexes to its maximum extent, it snaps closed in less than a 100th of a second. Yanega teamed up with two engineers from Cornell, Matthew Smith and Andy Ruina, to find out how. It turns out that the thin, flexible bone of the lower mandible gives it the same sort of spring as a diving board. The team used a mathematical model to show that the jaw deforms as it bends downward. The stress that this puts on the bone is stored as energy. Eventually the energy is released, and the mandible snaps back into place. Engineers call this process snap-buckling. Once again, hummingbirds are the only vertebrates to use it — but not

say, the short bill and broad, open mouth of a swallow or a swift). Nonetheless, even sicklebills (*Eutoxeres* spp.), whose grossly curved bills might appear to be a positive hindrance to flycatching, take insects on the wing. Hummingbirds make up for this apparent unsuitability with a muscle in the neck that allows for rapid sideways movements of the head as they turn to catch an insect, and a special feature, only recently discovered, that converts their bills into admirable insect traps. The key is an unusually flexible lower jaw.

the only insect-eaters. Snap-buckling also powers one of the most famous traps in nature, the insect-catching leaf of the Venus Flytrap (*Dionaea muscipula*).

Torpor and Frenzy

Hummingbirds cannot spend every minute of every day hovering in front of flowers or snapping up insects. The cost of doing so would be beyond even their highly efficient metabolisms. They need time to digest their meals, and to empty their crops for the next bout of feeding. Rufous Hummingbirds (*Selasphorus rufus*) have been recorded spending 79 percent of their day resting and 19 percent foraging. This is probably typical behavior. Amazilia Hummingbirds (*Amazilia amazilia*) in the Botanical Gardens of Lima, Peru, pass 80 percent of their daytime hours sitting on perches, and only 15 percent visiting flowers. The rest of their time they spend drinking, bathing, hunting insects and defending their territories.

Hummingbirds, by the way, are enthusiastic bathers. They bathe several times a day, either by splashing around in shallow water (even in water accumulated in a banana leaf) as other small birds do, showering in the rain or in the spray of a waterfall, rolling about on wet leaves after rain, or plunging repeatedly into a pool or gently flowing stream. After its bath a hummingbird may retire to a perch to preen its feathers with its bill and claws (the Sword-billed Hummingbird [*Ensifera ensifera*], which cannot reach its feathers with its bill, relies instead on its claws for its grooming).

Hummingbirds nonetheless live their waking lives at fever pitch. Their average metabolic rates are higher, and they use more oxygen for their size, than any other vertebrate. A hovering hummingbird may breathe 500 times a minute. Even a resting hummingbird may continue to breathe at 300 times a minute, 10 times the rate of a starling or a pigeon. To sustain this frenzied pace, its lungs must transfer oxygen to its bloodstream at an extraordinary rate. Its heart beats at high speed and at a high capacity, and its flight muscles replenish themselves with extensive capillary surface areas that increase the rate at which oxygen reaches their active fibers. At its highest pitch of activity, a hummingbird may need to get rid of some of its body heat. A thick layer of insulating feathers would get in the way, and that may be why hummingbirds have large featherless skin patches, or apteria, under their plumage and as few as 940 body (or contour) feathers, far fewer than for a songbird of similar size and the least known for any bird (most songbirds have 1,500 to 3,000 feathers).

A resting hummingbird, by contrast, has to conserve its energy. Small animals lose heat more rapidly than larger ones, and at night, or at times when food is scarce or conditions harsh, hummingbirds may not so much sleep as hibernate. They enter a state of torpor, shutting off or reducing as many of their metabolic processes as they can so that their fuel consumption drops to a minimum. Their breathing rate may be cut in half, and their heart rate may drop to 50 beats a minute. On cool nights the metabolism of an Anna's Hummingbird (*Calypte anna*) in torpor may fall to less than five percent of its basal metabolic rate, the greatest drop known for any bird. The ability to go into torpor may have been crucial in allowing hummingbirds to invade the higher reaches of the Andes, where temperatures may fall to near-freezing at night. Migrating hummingbirds may be particularly likely to go into torpor to avoid using up the fat reserves they need for their journey. By contrast, incubating females, which need to keep their eggs warm, only go into torpor as a last resort. Oddly, tropical hummingbirds (especially birds at high altitudes) may go into torpor more often than those at higher latitudes. This may be because hummingbirds enjoying the long days of a temperate summer have more time to gather food, and less time to lose energy at night, than in the tropics, where heavy afternoon rains can keep birds from feeding and day and night are close to equal length. For birds sleeping through a brief northern night, torpor may not be necessary.

Hummingbirds need enormous amounts of food. An Anna's Hummingbird weighing only $\frac{1}{10}$ to $\frac{1}{5}$ ounce (3–5 g) takes in close to $\frac{1}{14}$ ounce (2 g) of sucrose a day. Hummingbirds in poor conditions — the alpine cold faced by many mountain species, for instance — may have even greater needs. A hovering hummingbird burns fuel at a rate 10 times that of a highly trained human athlete, and reaches even higher rates when flying forward at top speed. Its flight muscles operate at such a pitch that they may be approaching the limit at which vertebrate muscles can function. They must contract, relax, and reload for the next stroke in milliseconds, and a hummingbird has to get energy to them as continuously and rapidly as possible. The time between taking on fuel (in the form of the sugars in its nectar diet) and delivering its caloric energy to its muscles must be as short as the bird can make it. Hummingbirds, as in so many other

aspects of their high-speed, high-fueled lifestyles, have special ways of dealing with this problem.

Their first tasks are to digest the sugars they have just eaten, break them down into glucose, and get that glucose out of their digestive tracts and into their bloodstreams at top speed. Some of it simply diffuses through the intestinal wall, but the active process that animals use to transport glucose out of their intestines operates at a faster rate in hummingbirds than in any other vertebrate.

Kenneth Welch and his co-workers have found that only 20 minutes to an hour after Broad-tailed Hummingbirds (*Selasphorus platycercus*) start feeding on nectar, they switch from metabolizing fats (as we do) to getting most of their their caloric energy directly from the sugars in nectar, converted into the glucose they have absorbed into their bloodstreams. This saves them the metabolic step of having to store the energy as fat first — a process that in itself requires energy. When we humans exercise we can get energy directly from sugars, too, but only enough to supply about 15 to 30 percent of our needs. Welch's hovering hummingbirds, by contrast, can supply three-quarters of their fuel requirements in this way. No other vertebrate can come close to this, but nectar-feeding hawk moths, insects many people mistake for hovering hummingbirds, can do much the same thing. Both bird and insect seem to have adjusted their metabolisms as they specialized for life as a hovering nectar-feeder. It's a remarkable example of convergent evolution modeling not just shape and form, but body chemistry.

Hummingbird Journeys

Every year Rufous Hummingbirds (*Selasphorus rufus*) fly the length of the Rocky Mountains, from Alaska to Mexico. Green-backed Firecrowns (*Sephanoides sephaniodes*) fly from Tierra del Fuego to northern Chile and Argentina to escape the austral winter. They can stop to refuel along the way, but Ruby-throated Hummingbirds (*Archilochus colubris*) cross the entire Gulf of Mexico in a single flight, a journey that covers some 500 miles (800 km). Long-distance migration adds a further burden to the already extreme lives of 29 species of hummingbirds of North and southern South America. One of them, the Calliope Hummingbird (*Selasphorus calliope*) is the smallest long-distance migratory bird in the world.

The ability to refuel quickly and efficiently is essential for any hummingbird making a long-distance migratory journey. Though a feeding hummingbird can fuel its flight muscles directly from sucrose, a migrating hummingbird needs fat. To supply its flight muscles a migrating Ruby-throated Hummingbird burns off its fat stores at the rate of two percent of its body mass per meter per hour, the lowest known fuel efficiency rating for any migratory bird. To rebuild its supplies it has to synthesize more fat, and it does so at an extraordinary rate. Over the course of its migration, a hummingbird may put on enough fat to equal 40 percent of its body mass.

A migrating Rufous Hummingbird can put on 10 percent of its body weight in fat in a day. That isn't easy, and we're still not sure exactly how the bird manages it. On their way south in late summer Rufous Hummingbirds refuel in mountain meadows where morning temperatures may be near freezing. Hummingbirds usually migrate by day, so a bird awakening in a mountain meadow has probably spent the night in torpor. It has to burn enough energy to warm up, and to keep warm in the cold morning air, before it can start to store fat for the next leg of its journey. It needs energy-rich nectar, but flowers that bloom at high altitudes tend not to produce nectar with a high concentration of sucrose. It will have to rest whenever it can to avoid switching from fueling its flight with sucrose to burning its fat. Metabolizing fat uses about 15 percent more oxygen than burning sugar, a real consideration for a bird in the thin air of an alpine meadow.

Studying the sugar and fat metabolism of migrating hummingbirds, by the way, may be of more than just ornithological interest. Raul Suarez has suggested that understanding how hummingbirds synthesize and burn their fuel supplies "may yield unexpected insights into the causes of human obesity."

The flights of the Ruby-throated Hummingbird across the Gulf of Mexico are, as far as we know, the only long-distance migratory flights for any hummingbird that must be made without a refueling stop. Ruby-throats arriving on the coast of southwestern Louisiana in April spend only about a day refueling before continuing on their way northwards. Rufous Hummingbirds, by contrast, may stay at a refueling stop for a week or two before resuming their journey. Like other migrating hummingbirds in North America, adult males tend to arrive a few days before females and young birds. Males arrive in poorer condition, with relatively less stored fat and flight muscle mass than adult females. Male Ruby-throats have shorter wings and greater wing-loading (that is, their wing area is smaller relative to their body mass), and the greater stress they may suffer in crossing the Gulf may be a price they pay for increased maneuverability and the ability to perform acrobatic courtship flights. On the other hand, male Ruby-throats are the dominant sex, and this may give them a refueling advantage once they make landfall. On Horn Island off the coast of Mississippi, arriving males take over the best feeding sites. Females are forced to refuel at poorer sites until the males leave.

Forty-two species of tropical hummingbirds also migrate, but for short distances only. Eighty-seven are known, or thought to be, altitudinal migrants, moving from higher to lower elevations with the flowering seasons. Some, such as the White-bellied Emerald (*Amazilia candida*) of Mexico and northern Central America, are migratory in some areas and seemingly resident in others. Others, instead of being regular migrants, may appear or disappear in different areas, apparently following the flowering periods of their food plants. Many hummingbirds in Costa Rica move upslope to breed in the flower-rich wet season despite cold temperatures and heavy rain, and downslope in the dry. We

know very little about how, or why, most of these birds make their journeys. Are wandering hummingbirds being forced to travel because there isn't enough food, or are they making strategic shifts to take advantage of the best flowering sites available? Are there other reasons for hummingbirds to migrate?

The Blue-tailed Hummingbird (*Amazilia cyanura*) of Central America appears to be a molt migrant. In Nicaragua, it breeds mostly in the lowlands along the Pacific Coast. From late April to mid-July, during the peak of the rainy season, birds in the process of molting their body and flight feathers appear in the mountain forests of El Jaguar, 4,425 feet (1,350 m) above sea level. This is the season when insects and other arthropods are at peak abundance, and the birds may be resorting to the highlands to pick up the extra protein they need for the costly process of growing new feathers. Molt migration — traveling to a new area after the breeding season specifically to molt, usually because food becomes less available in the breeding area — is known for a number of songbirds, and the fact that we only know of one molt-migrant among the hummingbirds may simply indicate that we have a great deal more to learn about them.

FIVE

How Hummingbirds Glow

When John James Audubon called hummingbirds "glittering fragment[s] of the rainbow," he was not only evocative but, in a way, accurate. Hummingbirds and rainbows owe their dazzling colors to the same thing: the abilities of certain objects, be they water droplets or iridescent feathers, to break up a beam of light into its component hues. The glittering blues, emerald greens and dazzling reds we see in hummingbird feathers when the light is just right are, in a sense, not really there. Let the bird turn a fraction of an inch, and the colors may vanish. Male Anna's Hummingbirds (*Calypte anna*) make use of the fact that the bright magenta of their gorgets and crowns does not show from all angles. When a male displays to a female, he raises his iridescent crown and gorget feathers, orients them towards the sun for maximum effect, and moves his head rapidly back and forth in front of her. The color she sees does not appear as a continuous patch, but as a series of brilliant flashes.

A hummingbird's iridescent colors are not based on pigment granules embedded in the feathers (as are, for example, the buff, brown and rufous shades on a hermit). They are structural, the consequence of the patterns of protein molecules in the feather's surface layers. Pro-

ducing them requires a series of layers, each capable of reflecting back some of the light that strikes them, separated by a substance that bends, or refracts, the light as it passes from one layer to the other. When light strikes a soap bubble, for example, some of it is reflected away from its outer surface, but some enters the film surrounding the bubble and is reflected back from its inner surface. Because the light is bent, or refracted, as it passes through the soap, the light reflected from the inner surface emerges at a different angle from the light reflected from the outer. Interference between the two reflected beams cancels out some of their wavelengths but amplifies others, a phenomenon called coherent scattering (as opposed to incoherent scattering, such as the random bouncing of light off independent air molecules that makes the sky appear blue). The result is an iridescent color. If we shift our viewing angle, we shift the angle at which the light we are seeing is passing through the bubble. This changes the interference patterns, and the color may disappear.

The film that creates our bubble, with its outer and inner reflective surfaces separated by liquid soap, is, technically, a laminar nanostructure. The iridescent layers in hummingbird feathers are laminar nanostructures too. They reside in the barbules, the side branches that run off the main branches, or barbs, arising from the feather's central vane. Instead of having only two layers, like a soap bubble or an oil slick, the nanostructures in a hummingbird's barbules have many layers. The more layers there are, the more times that the beams of light striking the feathers are reflected, the more wavelengths are amplified or cancelled out, and the more brilliant are the colors that we see.

The multiple reflective layers in a hummingbird barbule are made of the protein ß-keratin, while the refractive space between them is filled with a matrix of melanin granules, the platelets or melanosomes, that contain pockets of air. Melanin, besides refracting light, absorbs "extra" light that might otherwise pass through the feather altogether and be scattered by the tissue under it, interfering with the iridescent color the feather layers produce. The air pockets within each melanosome provide additional surfaces where light can be reflected, increasing both the number of layers in the whole structure and the brilliance that results. Because keratin, melanin and air have different refractive indices — that is, they bend the light through them to different degrees — which iridescent color the melanosomes produce depends on how thick the melanin is compared to the air pockets. Thicker melanin and smaller air pockets shift the color towards the red end of the visible spectrum, while thinner melanin and larger pockets shift it towards violet.

Why, though, should hummingbirds have iridescent colors in the first place? Why are some hummingbirds so much more brilliant than others? Why, in most hummingbirds, do only adult males sport bright colors or ornamental plumes?

Some of the most colorful birds in the world feed on nectar. When they drive competitors from flowers, bright colors form part of their armory. Hummingbirds with iridescent gorgets flash them at rivals as part of their aggressive displays. Because so many flowers bloom in bright sunlight, hummingbirds visiting them may show their iridescent colors at their best. That is probably why most hermits lack iridescence: they are birds of the forest interior, where the light needed to bring out iridescent colors does not penetrate.

However, the extravagant plumage of many male hummingbirds probably reflects competition not for food, but for sex. Because hummingbirds do not form pairs a female can select the best male, but her only guide may be his plumage, his displays or the quality of territory his exertions have managed to secure. Her choice may be crucial if she is to raise a brood with the best genes available.

The consequence can be an evolutionary race to produce more and more fantastic plumes, brilliant colors or extravagant displays to attract females or dominate rival males. Colors and display plumes may signal how suitable a prospective parent, or how tough a challenger, a displaying male may be. The structures and pigments needed to manufacture them take energy to produce. A healthy, well-fed male may turn out fine ornaments, or more brilliant colors, than a weaker bird. Their quality, and the vigor with which he shows them off, may convince a challenger to give up the fight, or a

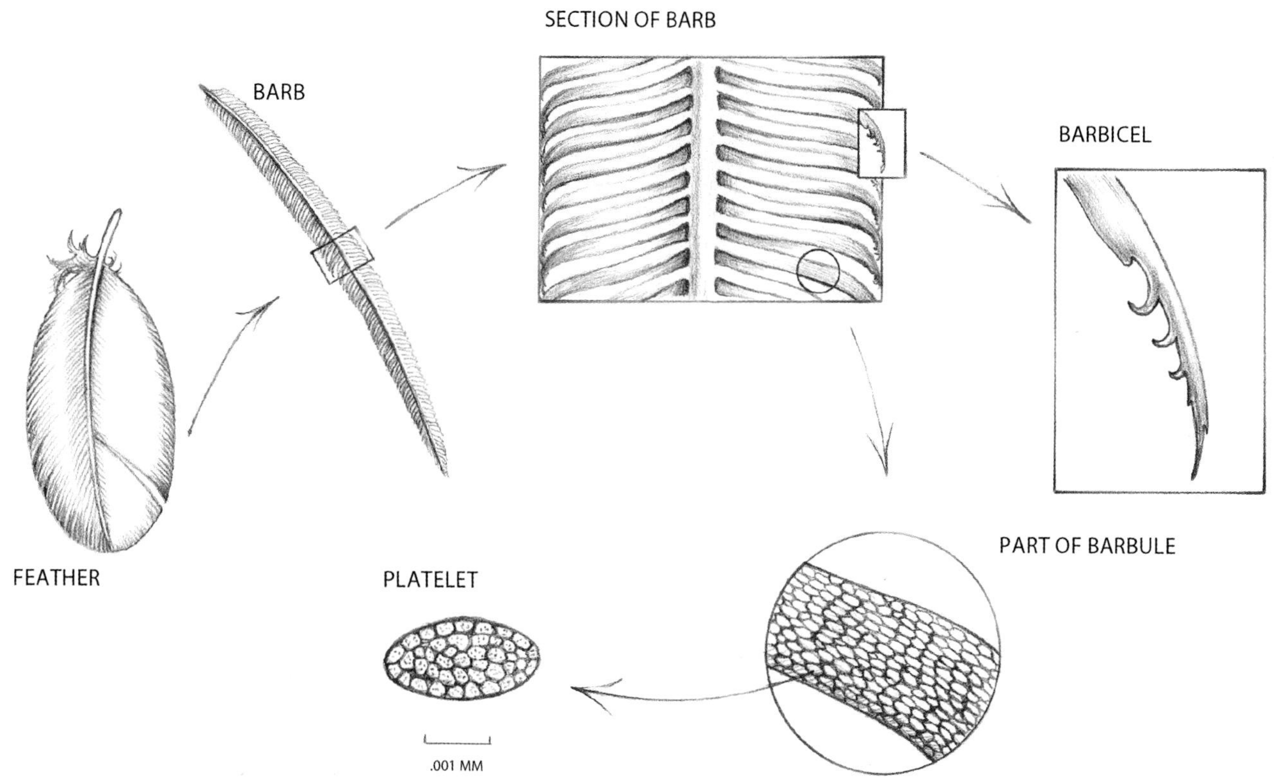

SECTION OF BARB

BARB

BARBICEL

FEATHER

PART OF BARBULE

PLATELET

|_____|
.001 MM

female that here are the genes she has been looking for.

Ornamental plumes, like the long tail feathers of many tropical hummingbirds, not only require energy to grow. By adding extra weight and drag, they may make it more difficult to fly. Christopher Clark and Robert Dudley tested this by the unlikely technique of fitting out male Anna's Hummingbirds with the long tail streamers of Red-billed Streamertails (*Trochilus polytmus*). When the newly ornamented birds were tested in a wind tunnel, the metabolic cost of their forward flight had increased by 11 percent. The extra cost may explain why migratory

hummingbirds don't have streamers of their own. For a real streamertail, a fine set of plumes may be a genuine mark — what scientists call an "honest signal" — of the genetic quality and overall health of the male.

Is the same true for the nanostructures that produce iridescence? Recent research has shown that these complicated structures assemble themselves as a consequence of their physical properties (think of the way a snowflake forms into complex shapes, by itself, because of the properties of water crystals). They take their final shape as the growing feather dries, after the

Hummingbirds owe their iridescent colors to the microstructure of their feathers. The melanin platelets, or melanosomes, packed into the feather barbules are filled with pockets of air, greatly increasing the number of surfaces that reflect and split beams of light.

cells that produce their precursors die. A hummingbird doesn't have to burn energy to build its nanostructures. Do iridescent colors give a female any clue about the quality of the males she is selecting?

Probably they do. Assembling nanostructures may be energy-free, but synthesizing their raw materials is not. Tiny details such as the amount of protein available to build up the keratin layers, or the thickness of melanin in the melanosomes, may have a direct effect on the brilliance and richness of iridescent colors, and may depend on a bird's health or condition. Hummingbirds need protein to synthesize keratin and melanin. Melissa Meadows, Thomas Roudybush and Kevin McGraw fed captive Anna's Hummingbirds on weak and strong protein solutions after plucking their gorget and crown feathers, forcing the birds to regrow their plumage. Birds fed on a high-protein diet grew more colorful crown feathers than those fed the low-protein solution. Their gorget colors were not affected, but a protein-poor diet can result in weaker and more breakable feathers.

Iridescent feathers may be particularly subject to wear and damage. Worn crown feathers on a male Anna's Hummingbird are much duller than fresh ones. The red gorget of a male Ruby-throated Hummingbird (*Archilochus colubris*) may become more orange as the summer progresses. As the keratin and melanin layers in its feathers are degraded or worn away the refractive index of the feather changes, and the colors it produces shift from the red end of the spectrum. The same thing could happen if a hummingbird is unable to produce the right amounts of keratin and melanin in the first place.

Why do some female hummingbirds — violetears (*Colibri* spp.), for example — have bright colors? Hermits aside, why are some male hummingbirds so dull? Why, for example, is the Sombre Hummingbird (*Aphantochroa cirrhochloris*) of southeastern Brazil less colorful than its relative the Violet Sabrewing (*Campylopterus hemileucurus*) of Central America? Have some hummingbirds lost the bright colors of their ancestors? If so, why?

We may never know. Male sunangels (*Heliangelus*) have showy, iridescent gorgets. So do some females. Others, even within the same species, may have only a few iridescent throat feathers, or none at all. In some parts of their range in the Andes of Colombia and Ecuador, most female Tourmaline Sunangels (*Heliangelus exortis*) share the bright purple and pink gorget of males. In others only some females resemble males, while in still others most or all females have dull whitish throats. Female Amethyst-throated Sunangels (*H. amethysticollis*) develop an iridescent gorget as immatures, but lose it when they molt into adult plumage. We don't know exactly why any of this happens. Since an iridescent gorget may serve both to attract a partner and to repel a rival from a patch of flowers, without a knowledge of a species' history it may be impossible to tell whether selection for sex or for food, or for both, has had the upper hand in its evolution.

SIX

The World of the Hummingbird

Territories and Traplines

I once watched a Festive Coquette (*Lophornis chalybeus*) drive a Saw-billed Hermit (*Ramphodon naevius*), a bird almost three times its size, from a feeder in Brazil (the hermit reacted as though it had been attacked by an over-sized hornet). Many hummingbirds put such aggressive-ness to good use, defending a territory where they can control access to nectar-bearing flowers, drive off rivals or court females. To discourage rivals from invading their turf they may adopt a sort of scorched-earth policy, emp-tying the flowers near the edge of their territory before moving on to more centrally located blooms. In tem-perate North America, male hummingbirds usually take over the best territories, leaving females to feed in poor-er-quality areas or to sneak meals from male territories when they can.

During the breeding season, some male humming-birds defend courtship territories that may, or may not, contain a supply of nectar-bearing flowers. Most of the large territories male Allen's Hummingbirds (S*elasphorus sasin*) defend during the breeding sea-son are well-equipped with flowers, but some have few feeding sites. The birds holding them must go elsewhere

to feed. What these territories are for is not clear, but it may be that the birds are guarding suitable nesting sites for prospective females. Male Chilean Woodstars (*Eulidia yarrellii*) in the Atacama Desert of northern Chile defend territories in dense thickets, often with few flowers. Nearby clumps of suitable flowers are not defended at all. Woodstar territories form part of a communal display ground, or lek. As in other lekking hummingbirds, the birds presumably defend them not to sequester food but because they are desirable places from which to solicit the attentions of females.

The size of a territory may depend on the amount of food available. It may be quite small where patches of flowers are rich and concentrated. Territorial humming-birds prefer territories where they can limit their forag-ing flights to under a minute, so they can fuel their bouts of hovering with the sugars they eat rather than burning fat. During the breeding season, Scintillant Humming-birds (*Selasphorus scintilla*) in Costa Rica defend terri-tories as small as 33 by 33 feet (10 x 10 m) in areas with thick patches of Fuchsia flowers, but as large as 82 by 82 feet (25 x 25 m) where there are fewer food plants.

Territorial hummingbirds generally guard their domain from a number of perches, often at the tips of

tall branches, at the tops of bushes or trees, or on powerlines. They may choose less conspicuous perches outside the breeding season. Though Green Violetears (*Colibri thalassinus*) rarely attack intruders, other male hummingbirds spend a great deal of energy repelling rivals with aerial chases and flight displays. If there is more than one hummingbird species in the area, dominant birds may drive their subordinate relations from the best spots. In the Chiracahua Mountains of southeastern Arizona, Blue-throated Hummingbirds (*Lampornis clemenciae*) may displace Black-chinned (*Archilochus alexandri*) and Magnificent Hummingbirds (*Eugenes fulgens*). In Colorado's Gunnison National Forest, Broad-tailed Hummingbirds (*Selasphorus platycercus*) defend territories during the breeding season, but in summer migrating Rufous Hummingbirds (*S. rufus*), en route to their wintering grounds in southern Mexico, stop in the area to refuel. Though they are smaller than the Broad-tails they are more maneuverable, and both male and female Rufous Hummingbirds are able to chase the resident birds from their territories and take over. Rather than stay to fight it out, the subordinate birds shift their attention to lower-quality feeding sites.

In species with small, closely packed territories, territorial aggressiveness can quickly grow complicated. Christopher Clark, Teresa Feo and Ignacio Escalante

The Napo Sabrewing (*Campylopterus villaviscensio*) is a little-known species. This male is showing his throat patch to good advantage, and, like other Sabrewings, he will display it when defending his territory around a concentration of flowers. Napo Sabrewings are large hummingbirds that feed in the understory of the montane forests they inhabit. Persistent deforestation of the forests is jeopardizing the survival of the species, which has been designated as Near Threatened.

recently reported that intruding male Volcano Hummingbirds (*Selasphorus flammula*) on the Cerro de la Muerte, Costa Rica, "would frequently fly onto another's territory. The owner would leave his perch and chase the intruder. The chase would often, due to the close packing of territories, immediately encroach on a neighboring territory, and that bird would join the chase as well; if the chase then entered yet another male's airspace, he too would join the fray. The greatest number of birds we observed in such a chase was four, accompanied by a tremendous twittering."

Male Purple-throated Caribs (*Eulampis jugularis*), perhaps uniquely among hummingbirds, guard the same clump of heliconias for up to five years. The birds defend the area around the clump only in spring, when the plants are in flower, but return to the same clump each year. They chase off intruders, including other nectar-feeding birds, but will allow in a receptive female for a visit that usually ends in mating. During the rest of the year the birds shift their defenses to other flowering plants, but they may revisit "their" heliconias even when they are not in flower. These visits may reinforce their long-term spatial memory, helping them to remember where the clump is in time for the next flowering season. This long-term program of aggressive defense may also reinforce the evolutionary bond between bird and plant. The plant depends on the bird for pollination, the bird makes sure that other species stay away, and this exclusiveness may have paved the way for the unusually close match between the flower and the hummingbird's bill.

Defending a feeding territory may not always be the best way for a hummingbird to secure its food supply. Guarding a territory, and chasing off intruders, costs energy. There may be a threshold point at which it costs more to defend a territory than it is worth. That can depend on the amount and quality of the nectar available, on the number of intruders the owner of the territory has to deal with, or on the amount of energy the bird needs to devote to other things. Green-backed Fire-crowns (*Sephanoides sephaniodes*) in central Chile were less aggressive in guarding their territories at lower temperatures, presumably because they needed the energy they would otherwise spend in defense to keep warm. If the cost becomes too high, hummingbirds are likely to give up territorial behavior altogether. In a patch of cerrado, or tropical savanna scrub, studied by Danielle Justino and her colleagues in Minas Gerais, Brazil, three species of hummingbirds, dominated by the large and aggressive Swallow-tailed Hummingbird (*Eupetomena macroura*), defended territories. Three others did not, but raided territories of the other species. If the experimenters deliberately reduced the number of flowers or the amount of nectar on a territory, its guardian often abandoned its defense of the area.

Other hummingbirds use a different approach. Instead of defending a territory, they learn, and follow, a route that can take them, quickly and efficiently, from flower patch to flower patch over a wide area. Because this strategy recalls a trapper following a line of traps, it is referred to as traplining. Whether a bird is territorial or a specialized trapliner depends in part on its physical features, like its size and the length of its bill, and on the way flowers are distributed in its habitat. Territorial hummingbirds tend to have short, straight bills capable of feeding from a wide range of flowers, and may live

in places such as temperate alpine meadows, where an abundance of blooms may make a territory worth defending. High-reward trapliners are specialists. They have long bills and concentrate on tubular, nectar-rich flowers. In a tropical forest, where flowers such as heliconias are more likely to be scattered over a wide area, it may be better to be a trapliner. Hermits, quintessentially birds of the tropical forest, are high-reward trapliners. Some cover hundreds or even thousands of feet a day as they follow their prescribed routes. A Sword-billed Hummingbird (*Ensifera ensifera*) may travel several miles, visiting each patch of flowers only once or twice a day.

Low-reward trapliners have short bills, and visit a wider range of flowers that offer smaller nectar supplies, often over shorter distances. Other hummingbirds are opportunists that may either defend a territory or trapline, depending on whether large, defensible clumps of flowers are available. Still others, including very small species like coquettes (*Lophornis* spp.), do neither, but sneak feedings on the territories of other hummingbirds while doing their best to stay out of the owner's way. Within a community of hummingbirds, some may be territorial, some trapliners, and others may shift from one strategy to another as the occasion demands. Of 15 hummingbird species living together in a community in the high Andes of Colombia, the most common, the Shining Sunbeam (*Aglaeactes cupripennis*), is an aggressive territory-holder. Others, including long-billed birds like the Buff-winged Starfrontlet (*Coeligena lutetiae*) and Collared Inca (*C. torquata*), are usually trapliners, while still others, including short-billed species such as the Green-tailed Trainbearer (*Lesbia nuna*) and Purple-backed Thornbill (*Ramphomicron microrhynchum*), shift between the two strategies. Females of many species may trapline even if their males are territorial. Most female hummingbirds are smaller than males (females do tend to be the larger sex in small hummingbirds, including most "bees," though male Anna's Hummingbirds [*Calypte anna*] outweigh females). Traplining may be a way for female hummingbirds to avoid turf battles with their larger, and more aggressive, mates.

Hummingbird Songs

Hummingbirds are more varied vocalists than we once thought. Both male and female hummingbirds, like songbirds, may give short, simple calls or longer, more complex (if, to us, rather tuneless) songs. The songs of 44 Anna's Hummingbirds (*Calypte anna*) that Xiao-Jing Yang and her colleagues studied in San Francisco were constructed from a repertory of 38 distinct syllable types. Each bird used from three to six types per song, repeating them over and over. The particularly complex song of the Wedge-tailed Sabrewing (*Campylopterus curvipennis*) of Mexico and northern Central America can include more than 45 separate syllables, delivered at a pace of five syllables per second. Clementína Gonzalez and Juan Francisco Ornelas identified 239 different syllable types in a population of sabrewings in Veracruz, Mexico. Most individuals incorporated more than 20 syllable types into their songs.

Which call, or song, hummingbirds use at any given time may depend on their situation. Male Amethyst-throated Hummingbirds (*Lampornis amethystinus*) give a chattering call while chasing rivals from their territories, a buzzy call while feeding, a series of whistles during aerial display to females and a complex song the birds sing while perched. Environment plays a role, too: Blue-throated Hummingbirds (*Lampornis clemenciae*), which often live near rushing streams, modify the amplitude and intensity of their calls depending on background noise. The songs of Rufous-breasted Hermits (*Glaucis hirsutus*) consist of varied sequences of syllables of seven different types, differing from each other in frequency, harmonics and modulation. They do most or all of their singing during the breeding season, and since they do not defend a territory, the purpose of their songs seems to be to attract a mate. Courting male Green Violetears (*Colibri thalassinus*) sing on their perches from just before dawn until sunset, leaving them only for brief bouts of feeding. The Sparkling Violetear (*C. coruscans*) adds a song, given during flight display, not heard from its near relative.

Hummingbirds learn their songs, something few birds, except for parrots and the vast array of passerine "true" songbirds, are able do. They have special areas in their forebrains, the song nuclei, that are active when the birds are singing. These song nuclei are very similar (though, probably, independently evolved) to the areas in the brains of songbirds and parrots that are involved in vocal learning, and they probably serve the same purpose. As in songbirds, parts of their vocal repertoires (particularly short call notes and gurgling, unstructured songs) appear to be hard-wired into their brains, but to increase and diversify their song vocabularies hummingbirds such as Anna's (*Calypte annae*) must listen to, and learn from, other birds. Since hummingbird fathers have nothing to do with their children and female hummingbirds rarely sing, young birds probably learn their repertoires from their neighbors.

Being able to learn new songs is only important if a bird's vocabulary is both complex and variable. It is vital for many songbirds, whose chance of finding a mate may be increased if they can sing richer and more varied songs than their neighbors. It is also important for birds that use song to advertise their presence to other males, and need to be able to distinguish between a familiar neighbor and an outside challenger. Learning from one's neighbors can lead to the evolution of local dialects, something well-known in songbirds but little-studied in hummingbirds. Little Hermits (*Phaethornis longuemarius*), Green Violetears, Sparkling Violetears and Anna's Hummingbirds are all known to sing songs that sound more like those of their neighbors, and share more syllables, than do those of more distant birds.

Birds have a larynx as we do, but their voice box is actually a separate organ, the syrinx. It sits at the point where the windpipe, or trachea, splits into the branches going to each lung. In most birds, that point is in inside the chest cavity (as it is in humans). In hummingbirds the split happens before the trachea reaches the chest, so that a hummingbird's syrinx is in its neck. It is operated, in part, by two sets of internal (or intrinsic) muscles, structures its cousins the swifts lack altogether. Unlike our own voice boxes, the right and left sides of the avian syrinx can operate independently. This gives birds the ability to produce "two-voice" syllables that combine sounds from each.

The songs of the Sombre Hummingbird (*Aphantochroa cirrhochloris*) of southeastern South America appear to be produced in this way, as probably, are the songs of many other species. Adriana Ferreira and her colleagues found that Sombre Hummingbirds make at least six types of call, some given by females at the nest and others by birds defending their feeding territories. Males also have a multisyllabic song, a high-pitched, piercing, vibrating whistle followed by a series of soft, fluid, rhythmic notes. They sing while sitting on a perch, especially at dawn. They also sing in a most unusual courtship display: a male grabs a perched female by the skin and feathers around her vent and sways back and forth, singing, as he hangs by his bill. The female, perhaps unsurprisingly, whistles a few times while this is going on. In at least one encounter this ended in "what appeared to be aggressive interactions."

Hummingbird Courtship

Swinging by the beak from her vent (while singing, or not) may seem a rough route to a female's affections, but not all hummingbird courtship is based on persuasion. Peruvian Sheartails (*Thaumastura cora*) aggressively pursue their females and, at times, females of the related Chilean Woodstar (*Eulidia yarrellii*), forcing them to take refuge deep in dense bushes. Forced copulation, sometimes with the "wrong" female, may be part of the reason why so many hybrid hummingbirds have been found (including one apparent cross between a Peruvian Sheartail and a Chilean Woodstar).

Booted Racket-tail (*Ochreatus underwoodii*)

Hummingbirds do not form pair bonds. Females build their nests and raise their young alone, and a male is free to mate with as many females as will have him — assuming that he can catch their eye, or ear, or both. To do that, he shows off his plumage, his voice and his aerobatic abilities, either from a display perch, an isolated courtship territory or at a communal display ground called a lek. Lekking behavior has evolved several times among hummingbirds. All male hermits that have been studied except for the Rufous-breasted Hermit (*Glaucis hirsutus*), and a number of trochiline males, solicit females at a lek. Leks allow a number of males to share high-quality courtship grounds, and provide females with one-stop shopping venues for prospective partners.

Each male using the lek defends a small territory within it against intruders, though territory boundaries, and the size of the lek itself, may shift as males come and go. The number of males at a lek can vary from as few as two for the Rufous Sabrewing (*Campylopterus rufus*) to around 20 in the Long-billed Hermit (*Phaethornis longirostris*). Males on a lek may either cluster close together or space themselves broadly on a widely scattered, or exploded, lek.

A male that spends his day at a lek cannot be defending a feeding territory at the same time. Most lekking hummingbirds are trapliners. Only two species that defend feeding territories are known to use leks, the Rufous-tailed Hummingbird (*Amazilia tzacatl*) of Mexico, Central America and northwestern South America and the Swallow-tailed Hummingbird (*Eupetomena macroura*) of eastern South America. Unlike trapliners, which may spend their morning hours, or even most or all of their day, at the lek during the breeding

season, these two visit their leks for only a short time, usually just before sunrise. Male Swallow-tailed Hummingbirds studied by Marco Pizo and Wesley Silva in Campinas, in southeastern Brazil, arrived at their lek, on average, 27 minutes before sunrise, sang for only 17 minutes, sat quietly for a few minutes and then left for the rest of the day.

The sorts of displays hummingbirds indulge in are linked to the ornaments the bird has available to display. Birds with iridescent gorgets or head plumes fan them as they face females or rivals. Male hermits, which lack iridescent colors or ornamental plumes except for their long central tail feathers, fan their tails and show off brightly colored mouth linings, usually red or yellow. A displaying hermit, by spreading the base of its bill, stretches the skin around its gape, allowing sunlight to shine through it like the pane of a stained-glass window. In the Green Hermit (*Phaethornis guy*) the result, according to the late David Snow, is "like the sudden flashing of a red light in the dark forest."

The truly marvelous display of the Marvelous Spatuletail (*Loddigesia mirabilis*) shows off the most extreme ornamental plumes of any hummingbird. The only well-developed tail feathers of an adult male are two long, wire-like plumes tipped with immense rackets (the other feathers are very short, and what looks like a pair of pointed plumes in the center of the tail are actually modified coverts). Thanks to a special arrangement of enlarged muscles attached to the plumes, a displaying male is able to swing and curve them forwards until they form a U-shaped frame around the bird. He starts from a perch, waving his rackets back and forth. As his excitement increases, he helicopters back and forth over his perch and then hovers around the female, his spread-out rackets held fully out and forward. The muscular effort required to bring these oversize plumes into position probably makes the whole performance one of the most energetically costly displays in hummingbirds. The bird can keep it up for only a few seconds.

Hummingbirds are such aerial creatures that it should be no surprise that many of their displays involve acrobatic flight. A male Plovercrest (*Stephanoxis lalandi*) challenging a territory-holder at a lek makes short, rapid back-and-forth flights just above and in front of the other bird, keeping its long crest erect as it flies. Male Amethyst-throated Hummingbirds (*Lampornis amethystinus*) display to a female by flying in a horizontal circle some 100 feet (30 m) across before plummeting past her, a performance they may repeat five or six times. Male hummingbirds in the "bee" group perform particularly challenging and energetically demanding flight displays. These usually involve near-vertical power dives from heights of 16 to 130 feet (5–40 m), ending with a high-speed, swooping arc past a hopefully admiring female (or, often, a rival male, or some other species of bird altogether — even courtship dives may begin as aggression). An Allen's Hummingbird (*Selasphorus sasin*) precedes its dive with a back-and-forth series of arcing flights (the "pendulum" display). Male "bees," in particular Ruby-throated (*Archilochus colubris*), Rufous (*Selasphorus rufus*) and Allen's Hummingbirds, tend to have shorter and more pointed wings than females, a difference that Gary Stiles, Douglas Altshuler and Robert Dudley argue is the result of sexual selection associated with their flight displays.

It took high-speed video analysis by Christopher J. Clark to reveal just how extraordinary these power dives are. As a male Anna's Hummingbird (*Calypte anna*) plunges earthward, he reaches a top speed of 60 miles per hour (97 km/h). As he swoops through the bottom of his curved flight path, he briefly reaches accelerations of 10 g, a figure unmatched for aerial maneuvers by any living organism except a jet fighter pilot. This rush of speed does more than simply show off the bird's flying skills. As he reaches the bottom of his dive, the male spreads his tail for a fraction of a second. At the same time he produces a loud chirping sound. Clark and Teresa Feo have shown that the chirp is produced by air flowing over the modified trailing vane of the outermost tail feathers, causing the vane to flutter in a high-speed equivalent of a flag flapping in a breeze. The sound can only be produced if the feathers are moving at a high enough speed to vibrate at the right frequency. The bird's dive may have evolved, in part, to achieve the necessary velocity, and a male's ability to produce a satisfactory chirp may be an important guide for a female seeking a mate.

O. T. Baron noticed as long ago as 1897 that the male Peruvian Sheartail flies "high up in the air and then comes down swiftly, making a noise with the tail like a ribbon in a strong wind." Such non-vocal sounds, produced by fluttering wing or tail feathers, are an important part of bee hummingbird dive displays. Competition for females appears to have driven their evolution and diversification within the bee group (though the sounds a Vervain Hummingbird [*Mellisuga minima*] makes during its display flights are, apparently, entirely vocal, and Anna's and Costa's Hummingbirds [*Calypte costae*] produce vocal notes near the bottom of their dives).

When a female Green-backed Firecrown (*Sephanoides sephaniodes*) builds her nest, she may be helping to spread the spores of the ferns and mosses she chooses as building material.

The outer, or in some species the inner, tail feathers of most male bees have been modified into sound-producing organs, variously narrowed, stiffened, curved, notched or unusually shaped in some other way, uniquely for each species. When the bird reaches the bottom of his dive and spreads his tail, sounds, usually tonal whistles or chirps, are produced either by the trailing vane, as in Anna's and Costa's (*Calypte costae*) Hummingbirds, or by the fluttering tip of the feather, as in the Black-chinned Hummingbird (*Archilochus alexandri*). The particular shape of each species' feathers determines the kind of sound they will produce. A diving male Allen's Hummingbird can produce three different tones at once, two with his tail and one with his wings. The male Calliope Hummingbird (*Selasphorus calliope*), whose inner tail feathers are broad, stiffened and subtly spade-shaped, makes both a typical flutter sound and a unique noise apparently caused by the tail feathers colliding with each other. He also adds a vocal call to the mix, producing a combined sound that only this hummingbird, and none of its near relatives, can make.

Sounds produced by the wings are more likely to be dry rattles than tonal chirps. The pendulum display of Allen's Hummingbird is accompanied by a chirruping sound made by the wings. A number of male bees, including Allen's, Calliope and Black-chinned Hummingbirds, make a rattling sound with their wings during close-up shuttle displays at the climax of courtship, during which they fly back and forth in front of the bird they are displaying to, with gorget flared to show its color to best advantage.

Male display reaches such extremes because, without pair bonds, female hummingbirds are free to concentrate their attentions on the most desirable male. Christopher Clark and his coworkers found that female Chilean Woodstars at a lek only visited, and copulated with, one of the males, completely ignoring his close neighbors. With only a few potential winners in the race to mate, the pressure for males to excel has driven their evolution into the bejeweled, frilled and plumed creatures that so many of them have become.

The Next Generation

Among hummingbirds, the entire burden of nest-building, incubating eggs and rearing young falls on the female. Raising blind, helpless altricial young (as opposed to the precocial young of, say, ducks or chickens, which hatch feathered and can feed themselves on emerging from the egg) can be difficult without a male helper. Birds that eat fruit or nectar are almost the only ones that manage it. For a female hummingbird, however, being able to do without the male has advantages. She has freedom of choice in her partner, and she can range through the territories of any number of males to find the food she needs for herself and her brood. Female hummingbirds are so efficient at going it alone that at least a dozen North American species may rear two broods in rapid succession. Some may start building their second nest before their first one has emptied. Females of seven species — Broad-billed (*Cynanthus latirostris*), Ruby-throated (*Archilochus colubris*), Black-chinned (*A. alexandri*), Costa's (*Calypte costae*), Broad-tailed (*Selasphorus platycercus*), Rufous (*S. rufus*) and Calliope (*S. calliope*) — have been recorded laying eggs in the second nest while still feeding large, growing young in the other.

Hummingbirds generally time their breeding seasons to correspond with the flowering of the plants they visit. When that happens can vary from place to place. In the north temperate zone most hummingbirds nest in spring or summer, though Anna's Hummingbird (*Calypte anna*), at least in California, starts nesting in November or December with the onset of winter rains, which stimulate the flowering of their favorite food plants. Farther north in southern British Columbia, where Anna's Hummingbird is a comparatively recent arrival, a more severe climate may force them to delay their nesting into Janu-

ary, February or later. Costa's Hummingbird may nest as early as January in the Sonoran Desert of Arizona or as late as May in coastal California (or twice, once in each place), depending on the abundance of flowers. In the high Andes of Ecuador, hummingbirds such as violetears (*Colibri* spp.) and trainbearers (*Lesbia* spp.) nest during the wet season, from October through March (as do many altitudinal migrant hummingbirds in Costa Rica and elsewhere). In Amazonian Brazil, by contrast, the Rufous-breasted Hermit (*Glaucis hirsuta*) breeds mainly in the dry season, from May to October.

Females of many trochiline hummingbirds — but not, apparently, female hermits — build their nests near a rich source of food. A female preparing to build will test sites for stability, repeatedly landing on a chosen perch or, in hermits, hanging from an appropriate leaf. Hermits normally attach their nests to the inside surface of a palm or heliconia leaf. To make the nest hang properly, a female hermit adds weight to the bottom, even weaving lumps of clay or pebbles into the nest material. Sooty-capped Hermits (*Phaethornis augusti*) hang their moss-covered nests from an overhead support, suspending them by a single cable of spider silk. Their nests have been found under bridges, or hanging from culverts and the ceilings of abandoned houses.

A female Green-fronted Lancebill (*Doryfera ludovicae*), a long-billed hummingbird from Central America and northwestern South America, builds a tall cylinder of mosses, liverworts and spider webs. She suspends it over a rainforest stream by a thick lip of spider webbing, usually attached to a rocky ledge or a clay bank. The nest has a shallow cup at the top to hold the eggs and young, and it may have a "tail" of material hanging from its bottom. Some nests hang free, like the nests of hermits but unlike nests of other species in the Trochilinae. Others may be partially supported by a ledge.

Most trochiline hummingbird nests are compact open cups decorated with moss, dead leaves and other materials, held in place with spider silk and lined with soft plant fibers or, sometimes, feathers or hair. Nests of the Collared Inca (*Coeligena torquata*) in northeastern Ecuador were tightly woven cups of soft, reddish-brown tree fern and bromeliad fibers, bound together with spider webbing and decorated on the outside with strands of light green moss, often forming a tail or skirt hanging below the nest. They were attached on the side near the ends of thin, vertical branches, at an average height of 5½ feet (1.7 m) off the ground. Females continued to add moss, fibers and what appeared to be spider webbing to their nests throughout the incubation period, and even until two days after the eggs hatched.

The Ecuadorian Hillstar (*Oreotrochilus chimborazo*) nests high in the Andes. Its young need protection from the harsh alpine nights, and hillstar nests are particularly bulky and well-lined with wool, fur and down. For added protection a hillstar may seek a sheltered site, often beside a stream where the air is warmer and more humid, and since these may be hard to come by a number of birds may nest in the same spot. Alejandro Solano-Ugalde found 11 hillstar nests clustered under a single concrete bridge in the mountains of northern Ecuador. Seven nests were still active, and the rest of the little colony seemed to have fledged their broods only recently.

Green-backed Firecrowns (*Sephanioides seph-aniodes*) are particular about the ferns and mosses they build into their nests. They confine themselves to a single species of fern, and a few kinds of moss, out of the many potentially available. The plants benefit from the bird's attentions. When the birds carry sprigs of moss and fern to their nests they carry the plants' spores with them, transporting them farther, and faster, than the wind might take them. As the nest dries it releases more spores, and the newly released spores drift into the wind from a higher vantage point than the plants themselves could reach.

Hummingbirds are rather predictable parents. Whether they live in the tropics or the temperate zone, they almost always lay two white eggs, nearly always with a day (or, if the nest is disturbed, even more) in between. A female does not start to incubate until she has laid both her eggs, so that her young hatch together. Once she does start, she incubates her eggs for between 15 and 22 days, spending (at least among the 10 temperate and tropical species for which we have data) between 57 and 77 percent of her daylight hours sitting on the nest.

Hummingbird hatchlings are blind, and almost featherless except for two rows of downy feathers, the dorsal neossoptiles, running down their backs. Once they hatch, most hummingbird chicks remain in the nest for a further 18 to 26 days. Nestling Green-fronted Lancebills stay in the nest for 29 to 30 days, perhaps because lancebills nest in unusually cool and damp surroundings. High Andean hummingbirds, exposed to colder and harsher conditions than species of more moderate climes, may take up to 40 days to fledge.

Female hummingbirds feed their young by regurgitating into the young birds' mouths. They bring food to their nestlings roughly one to three times per hour. Nestling birds usually demand food with loud begging cries, but most hummingbird nestlings, by contrast, stay largely silent until they are out of the nest. When their mother arrives with food, she lands on the rim of the nest and taps her chicks behind their bulging eyes with her bill. The baby birds respond to her tap by opening their beaks to beg for food, but they do not call. When the growing young are about six days old and their body feathers start to sprout, their dorsal neossoptiles remain attached to the growing feathers (see p. 95). When her brood is about 10 days old, and the chicks begin sitting on the edge of the nest cup, their mother hovers over them instead of landing on the nest. She also no longer taps them with her bill. Instead, her beating wings ruffle the neossoptiles, and it appears that this is what stimulates the chicks to beg. If the neossoptiles are removed from 10-day-old nestlings, they no longer beg when their mother arrives.

Begging for food without making noise is a good idea for tiny birds whose cries could attract predators or nest robbers. Baby sylphs (*Aglaiocercus* spp.) and metaltails (*Metallura* spp.) do call to their mother from the nest — but, as Karl Schuchmann has pointed out, these hummingbirds build domed (or, for metaltails, semi-domed or deeply cupped) nests, where their young may be less vulnerable to attack than the typical hummingbird chick sitting in an open cup.

A mother hummingbird starts out spending about half her time brooding her chicks, but as they grow their own coat of feathers she broods less and less. Female Violet-chested Hummingbirds (*Sternoclyta cyanopectus*) in Yacambú National Park, Venezuela, stopped brooding their young altogether after 13 days. Collared Incas in eastern Ecuador stopped brooding after only seven days. The young stayed in the nest, fed but unbrooded, for 13 days longer, and emerged from it slightly heavier than their mother.

Females take considerable pains to avoid leading predators to their nests, zigzagging or circling as they approach to confuse anything that might be watching. Fairies (*Heliothryx* spp.) leaving their nests glide downwards out of the forest canopy in a spiraling flight that may fool predators into mistaking them for a falling leaf. Nonetheless, predators robbed about three-quarters of the nests of Long-billed Hermits (*Phaethornis longirostris*) in Costa Rica. In Yacambú, predators robbed 40 percent of Violet-chested Hummingbird nests. Another 16 percent were destroyed by bad weather or lost for other reasons.

Young hummingbirds that do survive seem to start out with an instinctive urge to probe flowers. They may begin poking at promising objects while their mother is still feeding them. As they grow, they learn which flowers are best by watching older, experienced birds, including their mother. Learning from others is an ability that may stay with them throughout their life. Migrating hummingbirds in unfamiliar places may learn to find food by watching other birds. Their ability to keep learning, and to remember what they learn, is crucial in the extreme lifestyle that the young birds will have to lead, a lifestyle that will set them far apart from the rest of the avian clan.

SEVEN

A Future for Hummingbirds

Hummingbirds are remarkably resilient. We have lost surprisingly few, even on oceanic islands where so many species have vanished. Most West Indian hummingbirds remain common or abundant, flourishing in second-growth woods and urban gardens. The Giant Hummingbird (*Patagona gigas*) may even have benefited from the spread of colonial agriculture. In Ecuador and northern Peru it is particularly drawn to the flowers of agave, a plant first brought here, probably from Mexico, sometime in the 16th century. As the foreign plants took hold Giant Hummingbirds spread northward, possibly following this new source of nectar.

Resilience, though, has its limits. Today 54 hummingbirds, roughly one in seven, appear in the *IUCN Red List of Threatened Species*. Eight qualify as Critically Endangered, the most severe category of threat. Eighteen are listed as Endangered. Eight more are categorized as Vulnerable, and a further 18 as Near Threatened.

The remaining two, Brace's Emerald (*Chlorostilbon bracei*) of the Bahamas and Gould's Emerald (*C. elegans*), probably from Jamaica, are extinct. Each is known from a single specimen, Brace's collected in 1877 and Gould's before 1860. Some fossil bones from the Bahamas prob-

ably belonged, as well, to Brace's Emerald. Another hummingbird, the Bogotá Sunangel (*Heliangelus zusii*), is known only from a skin purchased in Colombia in 1909. Long thought (possibly correctly) to be a hybrid, it has recently been recognized as a valid, and probably extinct, species, based on analysis of DNA from the only known specimen. There was a flurry of excitement in 2011 when a living hummingbird photographed in southern Colombia was identified as the long-lost Bogotá Sunangel, but it appears now that it may be another hybrid. On the critical list are the Short-crested Coquette (*Lophornis brachylophus*), known only from a 15-mile (25 km) stretch of road northwest of Acapulco, Mexico; the Dusky Starfrontlet (*Coeligena orina*), known to survive only in tiny forest fragments in northwestern Colombia; and the Sapphire-bellied Hummingbird (*Lepidopyga lilliae*), restricted to small areas of mangrove forest on the Caribbean coast of Colombia and possibly only a color form of the more widespread Sapphire-throated Hummingbird (*L. coeruleogularis*). Four Critically Endangered pufflegs (*Eriocnemis*) are confined to remnant areas the western Andes of southwestern Colombia and northwestern Ecuador, where

Sword-billed Hummingbird
(*Ensifera ensifera*)

65

mountain forests are rapidly being destroyed. The Turquoise-throated Puffleg (*Eriocnemis godini*) of Ecuador has not been definitely recorded since the 19th century. Despite an uncertain sight record from 1976, it may already be extinct. The Black-breasted Puffleg (*E. nigrivestis*) is known only from a few mountains in northern Ecuador. Two others, confined to the Cauca district of Colombia, have only been known to science for a few years. The Colorful Puffleg (*E. mirabilis*) was first found in 1967. The Gorgeted Puffleg (*E. isabellae*), described as recently as 2007, has only been found in elfin forest habitat that probably covers less than 4 square miles (10 km²). Even that tiny patch is disappearing, replaced by agriculture and illegal coca plantations. The Juan Fernandez Firecrown (*Sephanoides fernandensis*) is now confined to an area of 14 square miles (11 km²) on Robinson Crusoe Island, Chile, where it suffers from destruction of native forests, the spread of introduced Elmleaf Blackberry (*Rubus ulmifolius*) at the expense of its food plants, predation by introduced rats, nest robbery by the recently arrived Austral Thrush (*Turdus falcklandii*), and possible competition from its smaller, widespread and more numerous cousin the Green-backed Firecrown (*S. sephaniodes*). There are probably only about 1,100 birds left.

Of the species listed as Endangered, the Chilean Woodstar (*Eulidia yarrellii*) survives in a few cultivated

The Critically Endangered Juan Fernandez Firecrown (*Sephanoides fernandensis*) is now confined to a tiny part of a single island, almost 435 miles (700 km) off the coast of Chile.

valleys in the deserts of far northern Chile. Once common, its population crashed after 1970. Today, perhaps 1,200 birds remain. Its decline coincided with the onset of pesticide use and invasion by a close relative, the Peruvian Sheartail (*Thaumastura cora*). The sheartail hybridizes with the woodstar and may compete with it, but the effect of its arrival is unclear. Key to the woodstar's recovery may be the restoration of native trees, now reduced to tiny patches and often eradicated by local farmers.

A century ago the biggest problem hummingbirds faced was the massive international trade described in chapter one. This was followed in the mid-20th century by another huge trade, this time in living birds, many of which did not survive the rigors of shipment or the difficulties of aviary life. The ruby crown and golden throat of the Ruby-topaz Hummingbird (*Chrysolampis mosquitus*) made it the most sought-after of all Brazilian hummingbirds by the international cage-bird trade until Brazil banned exports of wild birds in 1967. Before that, according to an 1883 guide to a hummingbird collection in the British Museum, it was "sent over to Europe in large quantities for the purposes of decoration of ladies' hats and dresses; and were it not for the extreme abundance of the species it would have been long ago exterminated."

The harm trade was doing was recognized in 1987, when all hummingbirds but one were listed on Appendix II of the Convention on International Trade in Endangered Species of Wild Fauna and Flora, or CITES. Today, CITES parties seeking to export hummingbirds, alive or dead (or hummingbird parts like feathers, or even DNA samples), must first make a finding that doing so will not harm their wild populations. Only then can they issue the necessary export permits. There are exceptions (CITES is rather complicated), including one for captive-bred birds. The Hook-billed Hermit (*Glaucis dohrnii*) has been listed on the even stricter Appendix I since 1975. Appendix I bars commercial trade altogether, again with certain exceptions. Trade is probably not a particular threat to this Endangered, but rather plain, species, but perhaps the added status is just as well; its habitat has now been reduced to under 195 square miles (500 km²), and there may be fewer than 1,000 birds left.

Much of the trade in wild hummingbirds dried up after the CITES listing, and after the passage of laws such as the Wild Bird Conservation Act (WBCA). The WBCA, first passed in 1992, effectively banned the import of wild-caught CITES-listed birds, including hummingbirds, into the United States. Hummingbirds are, nonetheless, still caught. In May 2010, customs authorities in French Guyana intercepted a tourist from the Netherlands attempting to leave the country with 16 hummingbirds of different species stuffed into pockets in his underpants. He was sentenced to six months in prison and fined 6,000 Euros (U.S.$8,565), perhaps half the amount he could have received for the birds on the black market. It was not his first offense: in 2008 he had been caught with 53 hummingbirds, but was reportedly let off after coming to an "arrangement" with customs. In May 2014 a Dallas man was indicted by a Federal Grand Jury after allegedly smuggling 61 dead hummingbirds into the United States from Mexico.

Despite continuing attempts to smuggle them from their homes, the chief threat to hummingbirds today is the loss and degradation of their habitat. This has been particularly severe in the northern Andes, where hummingbirds reach their highest diversity and where the greatest numbers of threatened hummingbird species are found. Climate change may make matters worse. Tropical Andean forests, now undergoing the greatest destruction of any hummingbird habitat, are likely to change drastically as global temperatures rise. Plant and animal communities adapted to cool mountain conditions may be eliminated, or forced to retreat to higher elevations. Coppery-bellied Pufflegs (*Eriocnemis cupreoventris*), once common at 8,530 to 8,860 feet (2,600–2,700 m) near Bogotá, Colombia, are now found only above 9,840 feet (3,000 m) and have disappeared from some lower forested hills. The more hummingbird habitats shift upwards, the smaller will be the area left for the birds to occupy. Hummingbirds living at the highest elevations may find themselves with nowhere left to go. As hummingbirds migrate up the mountain slopes, thinner air may place a greater strain on their ability to hover efficiently. A 2011 study by six prominent hummingbird biologists predicted that by 2080 hummingbird ranges in the northern Andes could shift upwards by 1,000 to 2,300 feet (300–700 m). Combine increasingly restricted range, forest fragmentation and the loss of habitat with the probability that plant and animal communities may destabilize as species respond to rising temperature by shifting at different rates, and montane hummingbirds are in trouble even if the physiological challenges of moving upslope prove to be small.

There is a positive side. In the 19th century, our fascination with hummingbirds almost led to their destruction. In the 21st, it may save them. Sedona, Arizona, headquarters of the Hummingbird Society, has been drawing tourists since 2012 with its annual Hummingbird Festival. The Peruvian conservation group ECOAN, working in partnership with American Bird Conservancy (ABC), has promoted the Marvelous Spatuletail (*Loddigesia mirabilis*) as a flagship species for conservation and birding ecotourism in northern Peru. Local children who once shot them with catapults now realize that the birds bring in tourists and their money, though the numbers coming are still small. According to researcher Nikki Waldron, this has "completely changed the culture. If any of the kids get caught with a sling shot they get teased by the other kids." Peruvian-based birding tour operator Gunnar Engblom calls the spatuletail "a fantastic poster species, the catalyst for conservation and nature observation in Amazonas Department and the rest of Peru."

Arrays of hummingbird feeders are a tourist draw at ecolodges throughout the Americas. Hand-feeding Red-billed Streamertails (*Trochilus polytmus*) at Rocklands Bird Sanctuary in Jamaica is a top-rated tourist activity. There may, unfortunately, be a downside to all this attention: a recent study at Cerro de la Muerte, in the highlands of Costa Rica, suggests that artificial feeders draw Fiery-throated Hummingbirds (*Panterpe insignis*) and other species away from flowers, even over considerable distances. The feeders could be having a harmful effect on natural, already-threatened pollination systems.

Organizations specifically devoted to hummingbirds and their conservation continue to be formed. In 2005, Luis A. Mazariegos Hurtado founded The

Hummingbird Conservancy (www.thc-fc.org) to support research and conservation efforts for Colombia's rich hummingbird fauna. The conservancy aims to protect important hummingbird habitat, and to raise awareness of the importance of hummingbirds with local communities. It has signed a Memorandum of Understanding with The Hummingbird Society (www.hummingbirdsociety.org), a registered U.S. charity dedicated to the conservation of endangered hummingbirds. In 2010 the Western Hummingbird Partnership (www.westernhummingbird.org) released an action plan for hummingbird conservation in western North America, designed to preserve the birds and their habitats for future generations.

All this is evidence that our love of these most wondrous of birds has matured. We now know that a hummingbird in its native home, or one drawn to our gardens of its own accord, is a far more beautiful thing than a desiccated curiosity in a glass case or a forlorn captive in an aviary. Today we go to hummingbirds not as collectors but as tourists, photographers, gardeners, ornithologists or conservationists. Whether they survive matters to us. As symbols of the natural world, and as warning beacons for the threats that world faces, hummingbirds are not just making the world a more beautiful place. They may, in part, be convincing us to keep it that way.

Violet-tailed Sylph (*Aglaiocercus coelestis*)

this glittering fragment of the rainbow

— John James Audubon
(1785-1851)

Hummingbirds

A Portfolio of Images

by Michael & Patricia Fogden

Above: Green Thorntail (*Discosura conversii*)
Opposite: Volcano Hummingbird (*Selasphorus flammula*)

Above: Purple-throated Mountaingem (*Lampornis calolaemus*)

Opposite: The spectacularly colorful Golden-tailed Sapphire (*Chrysuronia oenone*) has been described as "uncommon" but has a wide range that stretches from Venezuela south to Bolivia, including Colombia, Ecuador, Peru and Brazil. It inhabits lowland and premontane humid forests and secondary growth where the male can be territorial while the female is a trapliner. It is one of the many hummingbirds that have not been extensively studied, but authorities have predicted that the population is likely to decline because of the steady loss of lowland rainforests.

Left: Purple-throated Woodstar
(*Calliphlox mitchellii*)

Right: Purple-throated Mountaingem
(*Lampornis calolaemus*)

Left: Green Hermit (*Phaethornis guy*)

Right: The Brown Violetear (*Colibri delphinae*) feeds mainly in the forest canopy, frequently from low-reward flowers also visited by insects. Occasionally it will defend a territory where it is dominant over smaller hummingbirds. Although it is less colorful than most other hummingbirds, it has a small but glittering throat patch and will flare the violet "ears" after which it is named in aggressive confrontations with rival birds.

Left: Magnificent Hummingbird (*Eugenes fulgens*)

Right: Green Violetear (*Colibri thalassinus*)
The relationship between hummingbirds and most of the flowers at which they feed is symbiotic — the hummingbird feeds and the flower is pollinated — and efficiency is important to both halves of the partnership. The hummingbird works hard to find the nectar it needs and can't afford to forage where the supply is either exhausted or not ready. The already pollinated flowers of this orchid's inflorescence are not the same color as those with nectar. The hummingbird flies straight to the middle band of flowers, which still need to be pollinated and so are still producing nectar.

Left: Green Violetear (*Colibri thalassinus*)

Right: Ruby-throated Hummingbird
(*Archilochus colubris*)

Left: Although the sexes differ, both the male and female Gould's Jewelfront (*Heliodoxa aurescens)* have a distinctive orange breast band, making it one of the easier hummingbirds to identify. Even so, it is rather inconspicuous, as it tends to forage in the shaded forest understory and dense vegetation around rivers and streams. This species is named after the renowned ornithologist John Gould, who first described it.

Right: Black-throated Brilliant (*Heliodoxa schreibersii*)

Left: This aptly named Wire-crested Thorntail (*Discosura popelairii*) has a spectacular crest even though it is made up of only a few wirelike crown feathers. It has similar fine, elongated feathers at the outer edges of its tail. It is a tiny bird and is able to conserve energy at night by becoming torpid, lowering its body temperature like a temporary hibernation. It has been designated as Near Threatened as its numbers are declining because of deforestation.

Right: Purple-bibbed Whitetip (*Urosticte benjamini*)

Above: Crowned Woodnymph (*Thalurania colombica*)

Opposite: The Velvet-purple Coronet (*Boissonneaua jardini*) is considered by many to be among the most beautiful of hummingbirds. It has been difficult to observe as it favors the canopy of dense forests but will readily come to artificial feeders, where it can be admired more easily. The male displays his fine plumage during courtship by flying around a female and singing. Its range is restricted to the western slopes of the Andes in Colombia and Ecuador.

Green-crowned Brilliant (*Heliodoxa jacula*)

The male Magenta-throated Woodstar (*Calliphlox bryantae*) can aggressively defend his territory from members of his own species, but his diminutive size also allows him to filch from other, larger territory-holders. A filcher hangs around the edges of other birds' territories and feeds at the flowers when the owner is distracted elsewhere. Magenta-throated Woodstars fly in a smooth, beelike manner, and the hum of their wing beats is louder than other hummingbirds. The males also make distinctive wing snaps during their impressive display flights.

Left: Empress Brilliant
(*Heliodoxa imperatrix*)

Right: Collared Inca
(*Coeligena torquata*)

Above: Booted Racket-tail (*Ocreatus underwoodii*)

Opposite: White-necked Jacobin (*Florisuga mellivora*)
Hummingbirds lay two diminutive eggs. Sometimes the female begins brooding before the second egg is laid, in which case they will hatch in sequence. The chicks hatch after about 14–19 days, and the female has to keep them at a comfortable temperature. She'll sit on the nest to keep them warm, but she may also have to shade them from the sun if the nest is in an exposed position.

Above: Purple-throated Mountaingem (*Lampornis calolaemus*)

Opposite: Velvet-purple Coronet (*Boissonneaua jardini*)

Above: The Brown Inca (*Coeligena wilsoni*) is regarded as common in its range on the western slopes of the Andes in Colombia and Ecuador. It is almost uniformly brown but with distinctive white collar patches that aid identification. Its long, straight bill is well adapted to the tubular flowers it favors because it forages as a trapliner at elevations between about 3,280–4,265 feet (1,000–1,300 m) in cloud forests.

Opposite: Canivet's Emerald (*Chlorostilbon canivetii*)

Left: Brown Violetear (*Colibri delphinae*)

Right: Band-tailed Barbthroat (*Threnetes ruckeri*)

Right: Like all woodstars, the White-bellied Woodstar (*Chaetocercus mulsant*) is tiny and has an insect-like flight. While males will hold territories during the breeding season, they can defend them only from their own species. This species is opportunistic in foraging at all levels of the forests it inhabits and will steal nectar from flowers in larger hummingbirds' territories. This woodstar occurs in tropical and subtropical humid montane forests but also exploits degraded forests and cultivated land. It has a patchy distribution on the eastern slopes of the Andes.

Left: Green Violetear (*Colibri thalassinus*)

Fiery-throated Hummingbird (*Panterpe insignis*) males and females look alike, and both aggressively defend territories in the forest canopy. Both are also highly iridescent. Their iridescence is created by microscopic platelets in their feathers' barbules, which interfere with the light being reflected. The shape of the platelets determines how directional the resulting color will be. The body feathers of many hummingbirds show a green iridescence that can be seen from more or less any angle. The particularly intense colors of specific areas, such as a territory-holder's gorget, can, however, be extremely directional. The individual on the left is facing the observer, so the beautiful array of colors on its throat and belly are shown to good advantage. The individual on the right has exactly the same coloration.

Above: Green Violetear (*Colibri thalassinus*)

Opposite: Purple-bibbed Whitetip (*Urosticte benjamini*)

Left: Gorgeted Sunangel (*Heliangelus strophianus*)
Names such as sunangel, woodnymph, sapphire and
emerald reflect the appeal these beautiful birds have
for anyone who sees them. This species has a very
limited range in premontane forest on the Pacific
Andean slopes of Ecuador and just into Colombia. It is
not the sun lover its name might suggest though, as
it prefers dense forest cover. It is not well studied, so
little is known of its habits, but it is a regular piercer of
long tubular flowers.

Right: Booted Racket-tail (*Ocreatus underwoodii*)

Left: Only the male Booted Racket-tail (*Ocreatus underwoodii*) sports the spectacular, elongated outer tail feathers. Eight subspecies have been described, and their identities are differentiated by variations in the color of their "boots" and the length of their outer tail feathers. The identification of the females in the field is more difficult since they have neither of these features. This species feeds at all levels of wet forests and in secondary growth and is common throughout its range.

Right: Violet Sabrewing (*Campylopterus hemileucurus*)

111

Left: Violet-tailed Sylph (*Aglaiocercus coelestis*)

Right: This Esmeraldas Woodstar (*Chaetocercus berlepschi*) is a male in his immature plumage. Once he has molted into adult plumage he will be more colorful and have a brilliant purple throat patch. This species has a very limited range in the west of Ecuador, where its habitat has suffered so much destruction that the population status of the Esmeraldas Woodstar is now classified as Endangered.

The influence of the co-evolution of flowers and hummingbirds can be seen in the different lengths and curvature of hummingbird bills. A long, slender bill will give the bird access to nectar at the base of a long, slender flower and the extreme curvature of the White-tipped Sicklebill's beak restricts it to feeding at plants with similarly curved flowers. Hummingbird flowers, however, are visited by many different species and are probed by different lengths of bills so the relationship is not a hard and fast rule. The reach of a short bill can be extended by the long tongue or by piercing the base of a flower.

Above left: Long-billed Starthroat (*Heliomaster longirostris*)

Above: Coppery-headed Emerald (*Elvira cupreiceps*)

Above left: Violet Sabrewing (*Campylopterus hemileucurus*)

Above: White-tipped Sicklebill (*Eutoxeres aquila*)

Left: Booted Racket-tail
(*Ochreatus underwoodii*)

Right: Fiery-throated Hummingbird
(*Panterpe insignis*)

Left: Carnivet's Emerald (*Chlorostilbon canivetii*)

Right: Stripe-tailed Hummingbird (*Eupherusa eximia*)
Nestlings need frequent meals of nectar and small invertebrates to ensure their steady growth to maturity. This female is regurgitating a mixture of the two deep into the begging mouths of her young. The female will continue to feed her fledglings for a time after they have left the nest, while they learn where to forage by observation and trial and error.

Above: Collared Inca (*Coeligena torquata*)

Opposite: This Tawny-bellied Hermit (*Phaethornis syrmatophorus*) illustrates some of the characteristics that distinguish it from the more typical hummingbirds. Hermits have less iridescence and long, curved bills for feeding at flowers of a similar length. Both males and females of most hermit species look alike, and they often hold a very upright position, as shown here. They favor high-reward flowers and forage by traplining.

Stripe-tailed Hummingbird (*Eupherusa eximia*)

The Crowned Woodnymph (*Thalurania colombica*) is another hummingbird that has had confusing, and disputed, classification. The illustrated bird was formerly classified as a separate species, the Green-crowned Woodnymph, but is now considered the same species as the Crowned Woodnymph. To add to the confusion, different forms are known as the Purple-, Violet- or Blue-crowned Woodnymph. This species forages in forests, forest edges and cultivated areas such as gardens and plantations in Central America, Colombia, Ecuador and Peru.

Above: The Scaly-breasted Hummingbird (*Phaeochroa cuvierii*) sometimes holds a territory, but its large size also suits marauding, which involves stealing nectar from flowers in another hummingbird's territory. The Scaly-breasted Hummingbird prefers to perch rather than hover when feeding. It is not one of the showier hummingbirds, but its size and the white tips to the outer corners of its tail are distinctive and make it easy to identify. The males form courtship groups, known as leks, and sing loudly from exposed perches.

Opposite: Rufous-tailed Hummingbird (*Amazilia tzacatl*)

Above: Purple-bibbed Whitetip (*Urosticte benjamini*)

Opposite: Volcano Hummingbird (*Selasphorus flammula*) is among the smallest hummingbirds. Its bill fits into the narrow salvia flowers, and feeding on the nectar at the base of the corolla brings the bird's forehead neatly into contact with the flower's pollen-bearing anthers. During a subsequent visit to other salvias, the similar feeding position is likely to allow the pollen to be transferred onto the other flower's stigma, so pollination can take place.

Above: The Collared Inca (*Coeligena torquata*) is a trapliner, feeding at flowers on a regular route through its habitat. Its bill is well matched with the length and shape of the flowers of this epiphytic heath; hummingbirds with shorter bills are less likely to compete for the nectar of this flower. Such perfect matches, however, are not always available, so generally hummingbirds do not restrict themselves to a single feeding strategy.

Opposite: White-necked Jacobin (*Florisuga mellivora*)

Left: The Violet Sabrewing (*Campylopterus hemileucurus*) is one of the largest hummingbirds but is not as aggressive as that might lead one to expect. It inhabits mountain forests above 4,920 feet (1,500 m), where it is a high-reward trapliner that visits a range of nectar-rich flowers of the understory, such as this ginger. They disperse to lower elevations after the breeding season. The male's brilliant plumage makes him a spectacular bird, though the female is less so.

Right: Purple-bibbed Whitetip (*Urosticte benjamini*)

Above: Crowned Woodnymph (*Thalurania colombica*)

Opposite: Empress Brilliant (*Heliodoxa imperatrix*)

Green-crowned Brilliant
(*Heliodoxa jacula*)

Crowned Woodnymph
(*Thalurania colombica*)

Above: To create the lift needed to hover and maneuver with precision, the hummingbird's wings move in a figure eight, which gives it twice as much lift as the more usual flight pattern. Hummingbirds are able to do this because their wings are hinged with a flexible joint that allows 180 degrees of movement. This Green Violetear's (*Colibri thalassinus*) wings have made the forward stroke then rotated so they are inverted, ready for the backward stroke that maintains lift for both elements of a wing beat.

Opposite: Sparkling Violetear (*Colibri coruscans*)

Above: Black-throated Brilliant (*Heliodoxa schreibersii*)

Opposite: Snowcap (*Microchera albocoronata*)

Left: Booted Racket-tail
(*Ochreatus underwoodii*)

Right: The males and females of many
hummingbird species look different, and this
directly affects their behavior. In the case of
the Purple-throated Mountaingem (*Lampornis
calolaemus*), the male is pugnacious in the
defense of his territory and uses his iridescent
gorget to display and demonstrate his ownership
of a patch of flowers that he constantly patrols.
He is quite unusual among hummingbirds in his
quiet but pleasant song, which he uses to both
attract females and warn off rival males.

Left: Buff-tailed Coronet (*Boissonneaua flavescens*)

Right: Black-throated Mango (*Anthracothorax nigricollis*)

Above: Violet Sabrewing (*Campylopterus hemileucurus*)

Opposite: The female Purple-throated Mountaingem (*Lampornis calolaemus*) is less showy than the male, and although she is equally distinctive, she has less iridescence and is smaller, which means she is unable to defend a territory successfully. Instead, she is a trapliner, feeding along a route of low-reward flowers in the understory, many of which are also visited by and accessible to insects.

Left: Black-throated Brilliant
(*Heliodoxa schreibersii*)

Right: Rufous-tailed Hummingbird
(*Amazilia tzacatl*)

Velvet-purple Coronet (*Boissonneaua jardini*)

Left: Stripe-tailed Hummingbird (*Eupherusa eximia*)

Right: Most of the nectar hummingbirds consume is found in flowers adapted to the mutually beneficial needs of the birds and plants. Flowers are not, however, the only source of energy-rich sugars. This Rufous-tailed Hummingbird (*Amazilia tzacatl*) has pierced the berries of a hollowheart tree (*Acnistus arborescens*) so it can feed on their sugary juice. When nectar is in short supply, some North American species rely on the supply of sap made available by sapsuckers boring into tree bark.

Above: Rufous-tailed Hummingbird (*Amazilia tzacatl*)

Opposite: Green Violetear (*Colibri thalassinus*)

Left: Velvet-purple Coronet
(*Boissonneaua jardini*)

Right: Striped-tailed Hummingbird
(*Eupherusa eximia*)

154

Above: Green-breasted Mango (*Anthracocorax prevostii*)

Opposite: The Canivet's Emerald (*Chlorostilbon canivetii*) is a tiny and generally subordinate hummingbird that uses several feeding strategies to ensure a sufficient supply of nectar. It forages at forest edges and in plantations and gardens. As a low-reward trapliner, it flies along a regular route and seeks out small flowers with short corollas. It also filches from flowers in other birds' territories and pierces flowers to steal their nectar.

Left: Green-fronted Lancebill (*Doryfera ludovicae*)

Right: The changing range of some hummingbird species was among the early signs of climate change. The Steely-vented Hummingbird (*Amazilia saucerrottei*) is among those that can now find their favored flowers higher up a mountain slope, such as the Tilarán Range in Costa Rica. Those species that already occupied the highest altitudes, however, are now more restricted in their options, and many populations are consequently in decline.

Above: The Coppery-headed Emerald (*Elvira cupreiceps*) is found only in Costa Rica, where it commonly inhabits cloud forest areas. It generally feeds as a low-reward trapliner at small flowers, often those that are also visited by insects. The males tend to favor the forest canopy, while females are more often seen in the understory. They are altitudinal migrants that nest on mountain slopes above 1,968 feet (600 m) then descend to lower altitudes after the breeding season.

Opposite: Gorgeted Sunangel (*Heliangelus strophianus*)

Left: Empress Brilliant
(*Heliodoxa imperatrix*)

Right: Bronze-tailed Plumeleteer
(*Chalybura urochrysia*)

Bronzy Hermit (*Glaucis aenea*)

Some hummingbirds have restricted areas of iridescence with very directional visibility. The Empress Brilliant (*Heliodoxa imperatrix*) is well named though, as the male has allover glittering brilliance. The female's plumage is much duller, and the sexes also differ in their feeding strategies. They inhabit the cloud forests of Colombia and Ecuador, but the females prefer foraging at lower levels of the understory as compared to the males.

Left: The male and female Green-tailed Trainbearer (*Lesbia nuna*) differ. Although the female has a long tail, it doesn't even come close to the male's, featured at left, which is nearly twice his body length. The male enhances his display flights by making snapping noises with his tail. This species inhabits secondary growth forest, pastures, parks, páramo and scrubby vegetation at elevations above 5,577 feet (1,700 m).

Opposite: Little Woodstar (*Chaetocercus bombus*)

Above: Purple-throated Mountaingem
(*Lampornis calolaemus*)

Opposite: Scintillant Hummingbird
(*Selasphorus scintilla*)

Right: This female Straight-billed Hermit (*Phaethornis bourcieri*) does not look comfortable in her characteristic hermit nest, but it is the position females habitually take up when brooding. The female makes her nest on the underside of a leaf, to provide shelter, but she needs a large quantity of spiders' webs to hold it fast. The female does all the building, which can involve her circling the leaf while binding it in place. Unusually, this nest does not have a tail of dead leaves hanging from its base, as with most hermit nests.

Left: Purple-throated Woodstar (*Calliphlox mitchellii*)

Above: Green-crowned Brilliant (*Heliodoxa jacula*)

Opposite: The woodstars are among the smallest birds but have the loudest wing beat hum — the sound that gives hummingbirds their name. The male Purple-throated Woodstar (*Calliphlox mitchellii*) also creates mechanical noises during his display flight, thought to be made by feathers vibrating during his dives in front of the female he is courting. The species has patchy distribution in Panama, Colombia and Ecuador, but the population is thought to be stable.

Right: This Ruby-throated Hummingbird (*Archilochus colubris*) is feeding in its winter quarters in Costa Rica. It flies north in the spring to breed in eastern North America, ranging from Canada down to Florida, a journey for which it must put on body fat to fuel the long flight. This involves negotiating the Gulf of Mexico, either by the longer overland route, by island hopping up to Florida or by the most direct route — over 500 miles (800 km) of ocean.

Left: Velvet-purple Coronet (*Boissonneaua jardini*)

Left: Violet Sabrewing (*Campylopterus hemileucurus*)

Right: Green Violetear (*Colibri thalassinus*)

177

Above: Green Violetear (*Colibri thalassinus*)

Opposite: Purple-throated Mountaingem (*Lampornis calolaemus*)

Above: Velvet-purple Coronet (*Boissoneaua jardini*)

Opposite: The Violet-bellied Hummingbird (*Damophila julie*) can be mistaken for a woodnymph but is smaller. This species forages in low areas at forest edges and in secondary growth, and although it is not social outside of the breeding season, it can be seen associating with mixed flocks as it hunts for small insects that have been disturbed by the other birds' activities. It is found in Panama, Colombia, Ecuador and Peru.

Left: Coppery-headed Emerald
(*Elvira cupreiceps*)

Right: The head-on perspective of this perched Green-breasted Mango (*Anthracocorax prevostii*) shows the position of its eyes on the sides of its head. This positioning allows the bird to view a wide area behind it as well as in front and even above it, an important capability when keeping a look out for predators or rival hummingbirds. Hummingbirds are among a number of bird groups that have a second fovea, the part of the eye where visual reception is sharpest. The first fovea, like our own, provides sharp forward vision, while the second fovea enhances sideways vision. Having two foveas improves a hummingbird's depth perception, and its ability to judge speed and distance.

Chestnut-breasted Coronet
(*Boissonneaua matthewsii*)

Mountain Velvetbreast (*Lafresnaya lafresnayi*)

The hummingbird's wings are less flexible than other birds' wings, as the hinged arm bones that typically fold the wing onto the body are much reduced while the finger elements are elongated. The hummingbird's shoulder joint, however, is very flexible and allows maneuverable and hovering flight. Turbulence created by the action of the pair of wings can be seen in the ruffled back feathers of this Sparkling Violetear (*Colibri coruscans*).

Tawny-bellied Hermit (*Phaethornis syrmatophorus*)

Left: The Andean Emerald (*Amazilia franciae*) is most numerous above 3,280 feet (1,000 m) in Colombia, Ecuador and Peru, but seasonal dispersal to lower altitudes is not unusual. It forages around forest edges, clearings and scrubland. Both sexes are similar, differing only in the color of the plumage on their crowns, which tends to be bluer in the male and greener in the female.

Right: Fawn-breasted Brilliant (*Heliodoxa rubinoides*)

Above: Coppery-headed Emerald (*Elvira cupreiceps*)

Opposite: Preening their feathers is a regular and important occupation for hummingbirds. Most, like this Chestnut-breasted Coronet (*Boissonneaua matthewsii*), use their bill to keep their feathers in order and to remove parasites, but they also scratch-preen with their feet to get to difficult-to-reach parts of their plumage. In the case of this Coronet, its only inaccessible area is perhaps its head, as its relatively short bill can reach everywhere else.

Above: Western Emerald (*Chlorostilbon melanorhynchus*)

Opposite: Empress Brilliant (*Heliodoxa imperatrix*)

Left: There is a close, mutually advantageous relationship between hummingbirds and the specialist flowers they pollinate. The flowers that are adapted to hummingbirds tend to be brightly colored, tubular and accessible to a bird in flight and, most important of all, have a good supply of nectar. The heath flowers being approached by this Green-fronted Lancebill (*Dorifera ludovicae*) have all of these characteristics.

Right: Golden-tailed Sapphire (*Chrysuronia oenone*)

Above: Hummingbirds are likely to visit a range of flowering plants, but in order to be effective pollinators, they must deposit the pollen at the correct species of flower. This Bronzy Hermit (*Glaucis aenea*) has pollen on its forehead, and as it feeds at this passionflower that pollen will come into contact with the stigmas, thus allowing pollination. This bird has also been feeding at a heliconia, and pollen from those flowers is on its bill; this pollen will be kept separate while it feeds at flowers other than heliconias.

Opposite: White-necked Jacobin (*Florisuga mellivora*)

Left: Mountain Velvetbreast (*Lafresnaya lafresnayi*)

Right: In spite of their superb flying skills, if a hummingbird is able to perch it often will. Maintaining the balance between its high-speed lifestyle and finding the food to fuel that lifestyle is critical, so hummingbirds take advantage of any opportunity to conserve energy. Some heliconias, for instance, have bracts that form handy perches, but this Speckled Hummingbird (*Adelomyia melanogenys*) is simply hanging on to adjacent flowers while feeding.

Above: Esmeraldas Woodstar (*Chaetocercus berlepschi*)

Opoosite: Buff-tailed Coronet (*Boissonneaua flavescens*)

Left: Buff-tailed Coronet
(*Boissonneaua flavescens*)

Right: Purple-bibbed Whitetip
(*Urosticte benjamini*)

203

Left: Rufous-tailed Hummingbird (*Amazilia tzacatl*)

Right: The strongly curved bill of the White-tipped Sicklebill (*Eutoxeres aquila*) makes it well adapted to feeding at plants with curved flowers, chiefly heliconias. Even so, it has to share its preferred flowers with other hummingbirds, including those with straight or relatively short bills. Sicklebills belong to the hermit group and feed as trapliners through forested foothills, and they nearly always perch as they maneuver their bills into flowers prior to feeding.

205

Left: Brown Inca (*Coeligena wilsoni*)

Right: Gorgeted Sunangel
(*Heliangelus strophianus*)

Left: Chestnut-breasted Coronet (*Boissonneaua matthewsii*)

Right: The Scintillant Hummingbird (*Selasphorus scintilla*) is tiny and among the smallest of all birds. It is seen here visiting flowers that are not typically favored by hummingbirds. It is, however, characteristic of this species to forage at small, insect-pollinated flowers. It is a low-reward trapliner but also sneaks into the territories of larger hummingbirds. It occurs in Costa Rica and Panama, chiefly on the Pacific side, and breeds at mid elevations, dispersing to higher altitudes after the breeding season.

209

Left: Magenta-throated Woodstar
(*Calliphlox bryantae*)

Right: Empress Brilliant
(*Heliodoxa imperatrix*)

Left: Stripe-tailed Hummingbird
(*Eupherusa eximia*)

Right: Green Thorntail
(*Discosura conversii*)

Above: Wire-crested Thorntail (*Discosura popelairii*)

Opposite: As with all taxonomic groups, the classification of hummingbirds is under constant scrutiny. Some authorities consider the Western Emerald (*Chlorostilbon melanorhynchus*), along with the Red-billed, to be a distinct species, while others classify it as a subspecies of the closely related Blue-tailed Emerald (*C. mellisugus*). The differences are chiefly of bill color and details in the shape of their forked tails. They are all trapliners that feed at lower levels along forests' edges.

Left: Magenta-throated Woodstar
(*Calliphlox bryantae*)

Right: Empress Brilliant (*Heliodoxa imperatrix*)

Left: Purple-throated Mountaingem (*Lampornis calolaemus*) The day-to-day care of their plumage is common to all birds, as it is needed for insulation and streamlining as well as the all-important act of flying. Bathing is one way birds keep their feathers in good condition, and hummingbirds can often be seen plunging into streams or pools. Some enjoy a shower as well as a bath and take advantage of rain, as shown here, or the spray adjacent to a waterfall, and some even rub themselves against wet leaves.

Right: Violet-headed Hummingbird (*Klais guimeti*)

Left: Fork-tailed Woodnymph (*Thalurania furcata*)

Right: The Stripe-tailed Hummingbird (*Eupherusa eximia*) frequently pierces the base of high-reward flowers to steal the nectar (see p. 245), but it uses several feeding strategies depending on the conditions and so doesn't always bypass a pollinator's more regular way of feeding. In addition to feeding at hummingbird flowers it will also visit flowers designed to attract insects, as in the case of this passionflower.

Left: The spectacular bill of the Sword-billed Hummingbird (*Ensifera ensifera*) indicates it specializes in feeding at similarly elongated flowers. The bill is less useful, however, when the bird is preening. It is unable to preen anything but its longest feathers with its bill, but it has very flexible legs and feet that enable it to scratch-preen all of its plumage. It inhabits montane forests of the Andes, from Venezuela south to Bolivia.

Opposite: Purple-throated Mountaingem (*Lampornis calolaemus*)

Left: White-bellied Woodstar (*Chaetocercus mulsant*)

Right: Canivet's Emerald (*Chlorostilbon canivetii*)

Above: Feathers wear out with constant use, so to remain efficient flyers, hummingbirds replace all of their feathers yearly, a process that takes four to five months. During this period the hummingbird needs extra protein to grow new feathers and extra energy to cope with the added difficulty of flying without fully aerodynamic wings. The five secondary wing feathers of this Snowcap (*Microchera albocoronata*) have been shed and the replacements are still growing.

Opposite: Little Woodstar (*Chaetocercus bombus*)

Above: Hummingbirds fuel their high-speed flight with nectar, which they can quickly digest, providing a readily available source of energy. Hummingbirds can assimilate the energy-rich sugars in nectar in as little as 15 minutes and then eject the remaining fluid quickly rather than carry it around in their digestive system, as shown by this Magenta-throated Woodstar (*Calliphlox bryantae*).

Opposite: Empress Brilliant (*Heliodoxa imperatrix*)

Above: Purple-throated Woodstar (*Calliphlox mitchellii*)

Opposite: White-necked Jacobin (*Florisuga mellivora*)

Left: Magenta-throated Woodstar (*Callifphlox bryantae*)

Right: As with all hummingbirds, this female Purple-crowned Fairy (*Heliothryx barroti*) has the sole responsibility of rearing the young, including building the nest, which is a simple cup shape attached to a branch or leaf. The main structure is made of soft plant material and bound with strong filaments from spiders' webs. It can take as long as two weeks to build, so it is not uncommon for an old nest to be refreshed, particularly if there is a plentiful supply of nectar-rich flowers nearby.

Above: Although hummingbirds are particularly abundant in the lush vegetation of rainforests, they also occur in many other habitats, including arid deserts. Costa's Hummingbirds (*Calypte costae*) reside in the scrub and desert areas of the American southwest and southwest Mexico. This female is nesting in a paloverde tree and will likely have to forage over a wide area in order to find sufficient flowers to provide the nectar she needs.

Opposite: White-necked Jacobin (*Florisuga mellivora*)

Left: Band-tailed Barbthroat (*Threnetes ruckeri*)

Right: Green Hermit (*Phaethornis guy*)

Hummingbirds' amazing flying skills make them a difficult target for predators. Some small birds of prey are known to catch them occasionally, but hummingbirds are more likely to be caught out by flying into a window that is reflecting their habitat. Eyelash Pit Vipers (*Bothriechis schlegelii*) also wait in ambush among flowers or fruits, but even when taken by surprise, this Rufous-tailed Hummingbird (*Amazilia tzacatl*) was able to make a speedy escape.

Left: Magenta-throated Woodstar (*Calliphlox bryantae*)

Right: This female Crowned Woodnymph (*Thalurania colombica*) has covered her neat, cup-shaped nest with strands of moss, helping it blend into its surroundings. Moss is characteristic nest camouflage for hummingbirds nesting in the forest understory, while those that nest higher in the canopy adorn their nests with lichen. The building of the nest is entirely the work of the female, and, since her plumage is much duller than that of the male, her presence on the nest is inconspicuous.

Above: The population of this White-tailed Hillstar (*Urochroa bougueri*) is restricted to the western Pacific slopes of the Andes in Colombia and Ecuador. A closely related subspecies occurs on the eastern slopes of the mountain range. Both populations hold territories around nectar-rich flowers and favor hunting for insects over water. This is one of the larger, more robust hummingbird species.

Opposite: Green Hermit (*Phaethornis guy*)

Above: Sparkling Violetear (*Colibri coruscans*)

Opposite: The bill of this Stripe-tailed Hummingbird (*Eupherusa eximia*) is not long enough to reach the nectar in each long justicia flower, so the bird pierces the base of each flower's corolla and accesses the nectar that way. This is effectively stealing from the flower, as the reproductive parts are bypassed and no pollination service is delivered. Several hummingbird species "cheat" in this way if nectar isn't available by more normal means, while others, including the Stripe-tailed, make this system of feeding their specialty.

Left: This Green-crowned Brilliant (*Helidoxia jacula*) is extending its long tongue to reach the nectar that is secreted in the cuplike modified bracts of this flowering epiphyte. To feed, hummingbirds close the grooves of their tongue around a quantity of nectar, which they then squeeze off and swallow. It is a very fast action that takes place many times each second.

Right: Gould's Jewelfront (*Heliodoxa aurescens*)